"This book is a strong gestalt, a successful integration of theory and practice, of explanation and expression, into an intensely personal style of communication. Daniel Rosenblatt's precise and, at the same time, imaginative and flowing use of language in dialogue and metaphor makes exciting and enjoyable reading. It is the most painless and least superficial introduction to Gestalt therapy. I recommend this book to all serious students and practitioners of psychotherapy, as well as to the general public."

—LAURA PERLS

OPENING DOORS

**What Happens in
Gestalt Therapy**

Daniel Rosenblatt

OPENING DOORS
What Happens in Gestalt Therapy

PERENNIAL LIBRARY
Harper & Row, Publishers
New York, Hagerstown, San Francisco, London

To my past therapists and present patients

Contents

And, as the Cock crew, those who stood before
The Tavern shouted—"Open then the Door!
You know how little while we have to stay,
And, once departed, may return no more."

The Rubáiyát of Omar Khayyám
translated by Edward Fitzgerald

Introduction

When I first attended graduate school at Harvard in 1950 I told my professors and teaching assistants that I had been a patient in Gestalt Therapy in New York City. They laughed or expressed puzzlement. Gestalt *psychology* was a recognized branch of psychology, but there was no such thing as Gestalt *Therapy*. Fritz Perls and Paul Goodman were believed to be upstarts who were appropriating a distinguished name and ought to be sued for libel. I decided to bide my time and uncharacteristically to keep my mouth shut.

Now, twenty-five years later, I have decided my time has come, and I have opened my mouth. This book is the result. In it I have not tried to explain Gestalt Therapy—I still stand by the original work of Perls, Goodman and Hefferline. Instead, I am concerned with the concept of *style* in Gestalt Therapy. Laura Perls, Fritz's wife and collaborator in the development of Gestalt Therapy, has often stated that there are as many kinds of Gestalt Therapy as there are Gestalt therapists. What she means by this is that Gestalt Therapy is more than a theoretical body of knowledge. There is no way to proceed. As he works, each therapist develops his own style, which is in part made up of what he has assimilated from his own past; he uses it in a unique way that at its best is fresh, immediate, lively, exciting. It is part of how he maintains strong, creative contact with his patient.

What is enlivening for me about this concept is that as I grow and change, as I develop, so will my style of doing therapy. I can recognize how in the last ten years I have become more flexible, willing to experiment, ready to put aside conventional therapeutic wisdom, to risk more. I am willing to use my own past in a situation, to be naked, even to appear foolish, if it makes sense to me at the moment. So my style continues to alter as I alter.

For some patients this is a strain. They want a therapist who is more omnipotent, aloof, superior. At times I slip into these roles, but I would prefer not to. I feel best about myself as therapist when I feel freest to invent what will happen next, when I can throw away the rule book of what a good therapist does and does not do, when I can explore as creatively as possible what is happening between us, look freshly inside of me, look openly into what might be happening to you.

Other patients object for different reasons. They have read Perls in his later works, and they have come to me, expecting me to be a carbon copy of Fritz. They complain, "You are not a Gestalt therapist. That is not what Fritz would do." And they are half right. It is not what *Fritz* would do but precisely because I feel free to be myself, I can claim to be a Gestalt therapist. For Fritz did not have my background, nor do I have his. It would be inauthentic for me to work as Fritz did until I have taken from him what is useful and made it a part of myself. He would be the first to agree that I need to digest what I borrow from others. And so, for those who complain I am not Fritz, I agree. I have borrowed from him, but I have also tried to make it my own in my own style.

Now I feel stuck, and when someone I treat is stuck, when he tells me that he has nothing to talk about, then I ask him to try a small experiment, to tell me not what he wants to talk about but all the things that he doesn't want to talk about. I am always impressed with his list, and he quickly becomes aware from his list of where we can begin. We don't have to stay with his list, but we are free to get started and go on.

Let me try the same experiment and list all the things that this book is not. It is not a theoretical book on Gestalt Therapy, although I may refer now and then to theory when I want. There are enough theoretical books on Gestalt Therapy, and, besides, I want to do something different. What? We will have to see as my list proceeds. The book is not an academic book. I worked as a professor and author of research reports for more than fifteen years, and for the moment I have had my fill. There is no bibliography, nor are there any footnotes. My material comes from my own personal experience as a therapist.

This book is also not intended as a theoretical cookbook. I once considered *Throw Away the Rule Book* as a title for this book. I meant it seriously. Each person is unique, each situation is different, each Gestalt has its own intrinsic form. My task is to find out what is unique, different, intrinsic in this person, this situation; to explore what is special to this foreground and how it relates to this background. Since I am not trying to write a theoretical or academic or general therapy cookbook, I do not generalize at a high rate of abstraction, though the careful reader will find embedded in the figures such potential.

So, I am not claiming to be the ultimate repository of therapeutic wisdom, but I am aiming to describe as honestly as I can what I do, how I do it, what helps inform my decisions. At the same time, I am not writing an autobiography. My focus is not my life but how I practice.

This book, then, is primarily about my style and how I practice Gestalt Therapy. To accomplish this there will be some theory, some autobiography, some reporting of my therapeutic work, but my major emphasis is what happens to me as I treat, what happens to those I treat, and, insofar as I feel confident, how this comes about.

My wish is that whoever reads this book will gain some understanding of certain aspects of Gestalt Therapy in action, how particular principles of Gestalt Therapy are interpreted, made living, through my style as a therapist. What would please me would be if a therapist is encouraged to try new methods of relating to his patients and even to his own concept of what he himself is doing. I would also be happy if those in therapy are strengthened to ask their therapists to unbend a little, or if those not in therapy decide maybe therapists are human too and therapy is a risk worth taking. I personally found it so, and my life has been profoundly changed. One of my aims is to keep repaying this debt by trying to do the same for others.

Part One

INDIVIDUAL THERAPY

1 . You and Me

It is 8:00 A.M., and I await you, my first patient. *Patient?* A doctor has patients. A doctorate was conferred upon me, but I am not a medical doctor, and I do not want patients or to treat patients. I am a Gestalt therapist (Greek: *therapsis*—assistant, perhaps of the gods. As far as we know, the first therapists were Aesculapians, who dressed as gods at night and visited and anointed the suffering, while the afflicted slept in the temple). I want to assist you, individuals, persons, to become whole, to integrate (from *integer*) your lives. To do this, I need assistance from you, from the individual himself. You become my teacher and I become your student, to learn who you are, how you live your life. We become partners in an open-ended, free-wheeling venture to get to know each other, to assist each other. You (the other, my partner, my assistant, my antagonist, my friend, my enemy—who you are) change as our relationship changes, from minute to minute, from hour to hour. You permit me to practice my skills, to exercise my strength as a person, to feel good about my abilities; you help me to pay my bills. I help you to complete unfinished business from your past, to fill in holes or gaps in your sense of yourself, to learn, to grow, to have a second chance, to be reborn, to live.

It is 8:05. Are you late or is it my watch? I am never sure. Five minutes is something I am casual about, although you may not be. You say, Why did you keep me waiting? I got here on time and I expect you to be ready for me. I'm paying for this time and I want it all. My time is important. I accept your accusations, your self-righteous demands. I am not so prompt or so punctual that I can promise not to need an additional five minutes or so, nor will I be concerned if you are like me. This is the way I am. But are you aware of your anger about these minutes, do you know that you are all puffed up with indignation, and that your eyes are flashing? What are you trying to tell me about your feelings toward me at this moment? For what purpose are you using my presumed tardiness? To clarify what may be happening between us, I return to your *feelings* and not primarily the *content* of your statements. I am not terribly punctual, but is it only that which is fueling your fire at this moment?

So we begin our time together, with whatever is there, right now, at the surface between us. There is no program. We invent, improvise, create our script for today. Shall we talk about time, about anger, about being self-righteous, about being puffed up, about your spontaneous fantasy of quitting, about your posture, about your muscular tensions all the while this is happening between us? Or shall we not talk about these at all? Shall we focus on any one of these and have you try to experience it more intensely by exaggerating the feeling, by becoming more angry, by shouting, by puffing further, by deliberately attacking me, by making a case against me, by telling me how really rotten I am as a therapist?

Or shall we do none of these? Shall we drop this because something happened yesterday that upset you and you want to tell me about it, because you had a dream this morning and you want to work on it while it is still fresh, because you are bored with your anger and want to explore tender feelings, to see if instead of maximizing an opportunity to blow off steam you can reverse, see if you can try as a deliberate experiment to be accepting and loving about my limitations with regard to time? How do you feel when you deliberately fake your feelings and tell me you like my ability to be so casual about time, that you find me refreshing for not being so tied to the clock, that you admire my freedom to give or take five minutes in either direction?

You see, we are free to do as we please with our time together, to select side by side how we want to spend our time, to note what seems appropriate and then to stop and re-examine what we are doing, to see if we are avoiding anything, to notice if we are feeling so good about each other that perhaps we might risk seeking how bad we feel about each other. Our guide is the need to stay with what is happening between us, to see where this leads us, to circle back to where it has not led us, to invent what might have occurred, to try doing the whole episode over again, as if our past together this morning had not taken place at all.

In other words, we wander back and forth between now and then, between what is happening and what is not happening, between our wishes and our fears, between what is fact and what is fancy, what are our feelings (yours and mine) and what are our thoughts. This all sounds too easy. You say, life is not that simple, therapy is not that simple. I accept this. Why should you trust me enough to be so open? How do you know I won't take advantage of you, make you dependent on me, use my power to exploit you, hurt you, violate you, destroy you?

The honest answer is that you don't know whether I will do any of these, and our only hope is that you will *risk* some part of yourself in order to learn if I can be trusted. If I am trustworthy, then perhaps you will be encouraged to risk another part of yourself and then still another. A danger is that too quickly you will announce that you trust me completely and invite me to take over your life. Were I tempted, I might point out how flattered I am by your offer but still politely refuse. *You* and no one else are *responsible* for your life. I cannot accept responsibility for the life of any adult, except my own. To be responsible for my own life is as much as I can manage.

You test me. Can you smoke, drop your ashes on my Persian rug, put your feet on my coffee table? Yes. Can you swear, complain, bitch, *kvetch?* Yes. Do you have to be guilty about not liking your boss, your parents, your wife, lover, friends? No. Can you be angry with me without having to pay for it? Yes. Can you cry without being ashamed, humiliated, embarrassed, or embarrassing me? Yes. Can you fart? Yes, but I won't like it, and I'll tell you so.

Can you come late, forget appointments, be slow in paying your bill? Yes, but these then become subjects for discussion, just as they would be if you were always meticulously prompt about the same things.

Do I listen to what you are saying, do I remember what you have talked about, can I recognize the names of the important people in your life? I'll try, and I'm lucky enough to have a pretty good memory so that sometimes I even remember events that you have forgotten you have told me about. Do you have to admire me for my memory, bribe me with a compliment? No, I feel pretty relaxed about my memory.

Are you beginning to trust me a little? Good. Then we will raise the stakes. Can you call me at any time when you are feeling rotten? Can you cancel a session and not have to pay for it? Can you go out of town on business or for a vacation without having to account to me for it? Can you borrow small amounts of money? The answer is probably yes, although, depending on the person, we may have to talk about it.

Can you come stoned on grass, drunk on booze, high on speed? Yes, but I don't promise that the session will be worthwhile. I will ask you to accept responsibility for this, but I won't blame you or try to make you feel guilty about it.

Can you arouse me? Yes. Can you seduce me? I doubt it. I prefer to separate my sexual life from my life as a therapist. I felt the same way when I was teaching. It is too easy to make conquests among students or patients, and then when the sex is finished you will probably feel cheated and used. (Not everyone will agree with me, but this is my way.) So although you probably can't seduce me, I will admit I can be tempted.

Can you call me in the middle of the night when you are in great distress? Can you not pay me for months when you are out of work? Can you ask me for a reference for a prospective employer, a faculty applications committee? Yes, but we can talk about these things too.

I do not want to be mistaken for an all-giving, totally accepting mother-father. Sometimes my acquiescence is based on a one-time-only response, sometimes on the need to reach out to you, sometimes as a proof of interest, sometimes as a human gesture, sometimes as a calculated risk that you are not trying to manipulate or take advantage of me. You see, I take risks too. And if I make a mistake and you take advantage of me, then that is very useful for me to know. It is a costly way of learning, but I find it worthwhile nonetheless. And if you are interested, why, then you too can learn something from it.

How else can you test me? How else can I offer you my support? Can you touch me, stroke me, embrace me? Yes, just as I will do the same to you so long as we are both clear that this is not the prelude to having sex. (Are you sure, are you really sure? say the doubting Thomases for whom sex is so electric and overwhelming. Well, all I can answer is that both as a therapist and as a human being, I feel confident that I can convey when I am in a sexy mood and when I am being friendly, and I may be especially fortunate that no one was ever so deluded that he couldn't tell the difference.) Can you play with yourself, stroke your genitals, your breasts, expose your pudenda in a miniskirt? Yes, but I'll point it out to you and ask you what you have in mind. I will try not to make my question an accusation, but I will ask you to own up to what you are doing. I may enjoy your activities, but at this moment I confess to being stubborn. I have something else in mind for the two of us.

Do you have to tell me whatever you are thinking, whatever you are feeling? No, I will accept your right to privacy, even from me, but I will ask you for your reasons for holding these back. I want to understand what is causing you to withhold feelings and thoughts from me.

Will I tell you what I am feeling and thinking? Very likely, but I may ask why you want to know. I may tell you if only to please your curiosity, but I may also hope that by sharing my own thoughts and feelings with you that they will have some pertinence to your own experience at that moment.

Can you tell me your crazy, forbidden, unforgivable thoughts —that you want to kill your wife, that you want to fuck your daughter, that you want to go down on another man, that you wear dirty underwear, that your pet dog licks you down there and that you like it, that you never want to work again and have your father support you for the rest of your life, that you are jealous of your sister's success? Yes, you can tell me these and more, and I will accept them. And I may counter by telling you that you are not alone in these thoughts, wishes, fears. I may also encourage you to have a vivid fantasy with me, indeed performing in your imagination just the deed that is so frightening and desirable. Together we can explore some especially delectable grimy, grundgy and gamy detail. In other words, we may take your most frightening fantasies out of the closet and give them a chance to breathe and then see what happens to you and to them.

My task is to accept your thoughts and emotions without assigning blame, punishment, guilt, disgust, so that you become free to explore the wider reaches of their dimensions: what other thoughts and feelings they are linked to, what other fantasies they provoke, what we can do here in the office right now to elucidate them further. Suppose we re-enact in play the dread acts, with first you playing your feared-hated-loved-enemy-friend and then reversing and I playing the same part. What happens now, and how do you see the situation, how do you feel about it? What is new for you? How have you changed, if at all? And if nothing of any significance has occurred, well, then I have failed in this attempt, and I will try again. When I try a second tactic, and I still fail, and a third and a fourth, then I become suspicious and suggest that it is unusual for me to be so dense, and perhaps something else is happening.

Perhaps we are wasting time together. Perhaps you don't want anything to happen; you are still too frightened and threatened. Well, then, we are free to drop the topic and come back to it another time. Again, there is no need to assign guilt or blame. We tried today, and we will try again. I do not need to triumph in every therapeutic encounter, and you do not need to give up your defenses, your resistance. Instead, today we have both learned how strong they are, how you continue to block any exploration. Perhaps it would make sense then to explore your block, to give me a full description of the block, how it feels, what it appears as. Then I may ask you to become your block, to have a dialogue with your block, so that it becomes clearer to you, so that you become more aware of it, so that it is not experienced as something alien and apart from you, an unowned part of yourself.

But, you ask, isn't it dangerous to encourage too much trust? Won't I make you dependent on me, won't I become too important in your life? Yes, these are dangers, although from my point of view they appear in slightly different guise. I don't like dependent people. In fact, I don't even know if I know what the word means. I can tell you that I don't like people who try to find out my point of view so that they can mimic it, I don't like asslickers, I don't like people who call me up on the slightest provocation to ask my opinion. When I take a vacation I want to be comfortable that you will be able to look after yourself.

I also distrust your telling me how powerful I am, how you can't live without me, how I run your life. It pleases me to point out to you that if I am so powerful, will you kindly give up your bloody neurosis so that I can feel like a potent therapist who cures in double time. If I am so influential and powerful, will you flat out volunteer to work at charities I favor, give up smoking your foul cigarettes, get a Siamese cat to pet and love? No, of course not, only if you have decided to do so yourself. Well, so much, then, for my great power and your helpless dependence.

The only power I have is that which you choose to give me, of your own volition. Let us both be clear on that. I have enough trouble just trying to see if you are willing to trust me without having to worry about my turning your whole life upside down against your will. I think that this is an interesting idea to explore in detail, but I cannot give it much credence in my experience with you. Me, I am happy if I can get you to look at me, to listen to what I am saying, to reflect on it, to chew it over and see if it makes sense and, if so, why, then to try some of it out in your life. And I should add that I am delighted if I, this powerful person, can get you to pay your bill nearly on time.

But, you protest, you do listen to what I say and pay attention to it. Good. For isn't that why you come to see me, to hear what I have to say? Yet, what if you can flatter me by listening too eagerly to what I have to say and then immediately putting it into action, if you quote me back to myself full of love and wonder? Then I must be smart enough not to play the fool and point out what you are doing. I honestly don't need cheap flattery or imitation.

Well, then, you protest, what happens to the transference, for you are educated and have read a book or two. In fact, you probably have seen a therapist or two before me, since until recently Gestalt Therapy usually recruited its adherents from among those who had already tried some other form of psychotherapy and been disappointed. This was true in my case. I had visited a psychoanalyst five times a week for two and one half years. While I don't feel the experience harmed me, I don't think it benefited me either. I can hardly remember many of my 650 sessions. On the other hand, I can easily remember my sessions with Laura Perls and Isadore From, my Gestalt therapists. My Gestalt sessions were always (yes, in this instance I can use that ultimate word *always*) lively, full of excitement and interest. I particularly remember the vivid impression of these two therapists, being there, trying to connect, offering suggestions, feelings, personal experience. But then I don't think of Laura and Isadore as only my former therapists but as bright, exciting, lively, warm people. They didn't try to hide themselves from me so that I would develop a stronger transference, based on my own projections. No, I would find other ways of projecting if I had to. I also had as a counter to my projections my own strong perceptions of these exceptional individuals.

So you say, "Aha, he has an unresolved transference to his previous therapists, and probably he is trapped by the same limitation in working with me." Well, that is one way of looking at the situation. If everything, if every experience must be viewed in terms of some other experience, well, then it would make sense to interpret whatever is said in terms of something else. Still, you would have to account for the fact that I do not like all Gestalt therapists, that I have worked with other therapists in workshop situations, and I do not have the same feelings for these other therapists. Can you at least permit the possibility that my view of Laura and Isadore is based not only on my former experience as a trainee but also on what others who are not patients or trainees see in them? I wish that you might have the opportunity to meet them for yourself and then judge.

I try to be interesting and lively. In my own way. These are important words, for if I swallow Laura and Isadore, then I have lost part of myself until I can assimilate what I have taken from them. I need to make this part my own. If I become a replica of them, then I abuse us both and them as well. My task, just as it is yours, is to take from a therapist that which nourishes me and to digest it, to destroy it (to reduce it to small bites) so that I become a part of it and it becomes a part of me. Then it is mine, and I have produced a new form that is no longer a miniature swallowed Isadore or Laura.

Thus, you are free to take, borrow or steal any parts of me with which you may want to experiment. At first you will probably feel awkward and clumsy with them. Good. Any new activity or growth usually begins with a period of awkwardness or clumsiness. You may feel embarrassed or strange. Good. To risk embarrassment and novelty often leads to new behavior or awareness. Then you must stay with the new sense of something foreign that has been added until you gradually forget about it so that it becomes as comfortable as an old shoe, your characteristic way of walking or talking. (Of course, at one point or another during the course of your therapy I may ask you to pay special attention to your manner of walking or talking. But that is another matter, and we will talk about that at another time.)

Let us be clear, then. I try to be as much myself as I can in our sessions. I want you to respond to me. I am not your father-mother-brother, etc., etc. I don't want to be nor do I want to encourage you to think that I am. If you have some important unfinished business with them, I am sure you will bring it into our sessions. You don't need to confuse me with your "significant others" in order to do so. I can rely on you to do it fairly naturally with me. If you counter that the more I remain myself, the less opportunity it gives you to use me as a blank page to project on, well, I can answer that the more I make myself unreal and a blank page, the less opportunity you will have to encounter a real person. If you can't work through all of your problems with me, my guess is that you can do a better job with me being me than you could with my acting in a limited, repetitive, stereotyped way as a blank page. A blank page has just so many uses. At some time I would have to come out with parts of myself, and why should we both fool ourselves that by acting as a blank I am not revealing myself? There is still the location of my office, my blank neutral furnishings, my blank voice, my blank clothes. Doesn't all of this blankness have any effect on you? Don't you want to shout? As for me, I am too selfish to give up that much of myself to the concept of transference as to turn myself into that kind of dummy. No, you will have to put up with me, warts and all. And it is my conviction that we will both be better off for it.

You protest. You don't want to know about me. You want to keep me a shadowy figure. That way, I can be of greater service, as a remote benevolent doctor, as a skilled technician. Then I want to know why you want to reduce me to that. What is your need to isolate me to so small a figure? How is it that you are so willing to tell me about yourself but are unwilling to know about me? Have you been swallowing psychoanalytic ideas? Where is your natural curiosity? Do you prefer to make me up out of whole cloth, to say who I am without any data? All right, now I would ask you to invent me. Right now, tell me who you think I am, what kind of life I lead. Take a blank page and fill it in, but deliberately, as an experiment. You see, we can utilize the blank page too, if we want to, and in our own way. Not so that I force you through my blankness, in an unaware way, to complete the picture of me, but deliberately as a measure of your creativity, as a full participant, as an active, responsible partner, to complete your picture of me, to see what we can learn about you and your needs. Yet here you are not being misled but join me in an open way to explore me in this way.

Now, let us look at your creation. I am a sweet, gentle man, always ready to help others. Too saccharine a view of me. Perhaps you feel you need to placate me, to believe in a passive, paternal figure. Wait, you see me as a strong, controlling figure, eager to dominate others, even if for their own good. Then perhaps you are afraid of authority or perhaps you want me to exercise more of it. Which is it? You see me as a grasping, manipulative Jew. Then surely you must be angry with me, but about what? You see me as a tender, loving, soothing person. But surely you must be confusing me with some kind of ideal therapist you would like who will avoid confronting you with your problems. You see me as a boring, stuffy, pretentious windbag.

Ah, well, I'll buy some of the windbag, but as for the rest I must ask you to consider if it is yourself or someone close to you with whom you have me confused.

Perhaps you are right, after all. Maybe I am boring. Right now I myself feel tired of talking. Let us just sit quietly for a few minutes and let us see how that is.

Now barely a minute has passed and you appear nervous and anxious. Are you aware how your eyes are darting about, looking in all directions, how you pull at your mouth with your fingers. No? Then please do not interrupt this just because I have called these things to your attention. Please continue. What does that feel like? You're not sure; then continue doing it, only heighten it. Now how do you feel, what are you thinking? You say that when you pay attention to your eyes you feel that you are looking for an escape, an opportunity to find something out there to talk about; you also say that when you pull at your lip you feel critical, that you are thinking, judging what will be worth talking about. Well, suppose we let your darting eyes talk to your picked-at mouth. Have a dialogue, right now, if you would, between these two parts of yourself. Let us see what emerges.

You feel foolish. All right. Let us accept that and go on from there. Permit yourself to be foolish and to continue. Good. Now what has emerged? Your picked-at mouth pursues your darting eyes. The eyes protest and complain; they refuse to be criticized. Your mouth continues to blame, but your eyes rebel. They refuse to listen; they refuse to continue darting. They make a stand and stop darting. Your mouth stops picking. You are at peace for the moment.

How often do you engage in a similar war within yourself? Don't answer me now, but can you pay attention in the future to those moments when one part of you picks at, blames another part of you that is intimidated by the other part? Who are these parts? Can you hold similar dialogues with your warring parts so that you come to see them better, so that you attempt to resolve them by yourself?

Have you been aware of how you have been breathing while all of this was taking place? No, well, would you please attend to your breathing now, tell me how you are breathing. Let me answer that question later. First, see how you are breathing.

You tell me that your breathing is shallow, that it comes in small gulps, that it stays in your chest. You also say that you feel your chest is constricted, as though your rib cage were indeed a cage, tightly holding in your breath. Let me ask you to exaggerate this manner of breathing, to gulp your breath in quicker, shallower rhythm. Good. Now you tell me that you begin to feel a little dizzy, a little anxious. Fine. Now let me ask you to reverse your breathing. Slow it down. Push your breath out, all the way down to your abdomen, and completely flatten your stomach against the walls of your abdomen. No, you don't have to inhale deliberately. By just pushing all the air out of your stomach you will automatically inhale, filling yourself with a deep breath. Now how do you feel? Much better. Now perhaps you can answer your earlier question about what difference breathing makes. If you want to make yourself deliberately anxious, then breathe short, shallow gulps of air. And if you want to give yourself support so that you can attend to what is necessary, then see that you are breathing from your abdomen. But wait, what has just happened to your breathing? While I was just talking you stopped breathing entirely. Now what did I just say about breathing? You cannot remember. Well, that is an old trick—not to let anything in, to stop listening and to stop breathing. Perhaps this is your way of saying that you have had enough for one day. I too feel finished, so let us stop here and begin again next week at the same time.

2 . You Are Not Your Diagnosis .

What about diagnosis? Well, what about it? A diagnosis is a limited way of reducing a person to a concept. To call a person a schizophrenic, an obsessive or a character disorder tells me little more than if you were to call him a father, an uncle, a worker or a friend. Less, as a matter of fact, for one clinician's schizophrenic is another man's hysteric; one clinician's obsessive is another man's blocked habit pattern; one clinician's character disorder is another man's perversion, which is simply another man's pleasure.

I find it infinitely more useful as a therapist to think in much smaller pieces of behavior—what are you doing right now, how am I responding right now, what are you feeling right now, what are you thinking right now? If I proceed in an atheoretical manner, holding off global diagnoses, then I am in a much better place to be of use to you, right now, at this very moment.

Right now, then, I want to discuss "diagnosis" and the way Gestalt Therapy differs from other forms of therapy. To illustrate these differences I would like to refer to brief episodes in working with different individuals. However, I do not want to invent names here. I find myself rebelling if I use false names like Harry, Susan, Thomas or Liza. From my point of view a false sense of intimacy and truth is created, and I want to avoid this. Further, these thumbnail sketches (Mary is an attractive thirty-eight-year-old schoolteacher who has never been married . . .)

give a phony sense of now, look, I am telling you, the reader, what is important about this person; I am tipping you off as to what it is critical to know. Therefore, I would rather not use names or age or even sex in identifying the persons I want to write about. Of course, as I use personal pronouns, sex is revealed, and that is permissible. After all, my point is not obfuscation but avoiding a phony sense of immediacy, intimacy and "telling all."

What I want to do in this chapter is to focus not on individuals or personality but on aspects of the therapeutic relationship that exists between us. I am not writing about real people here; I am using a fragment of what is happening between us as a means of illustrating not his psychodynamics but the different means by which a Gestalt therapist deals with the situation.

Later on I will use names and other means of identification, but please be aware that I am not telling all that is important then or that you are knowledgeable about the person; but try to look on the information as limited tags, useful just for this moment.

Let me begin with Lon, an abbreviation for loneliness. Lon's husband has run off with her best friend. I find little value in diagnosing Lon as a passive, latent homosexual, a withdrawn, isolated, angry woman, out of touch with her anger and living in fantasy. Instead, I find it much more useful to feel Lon's pain, to offer her sympathy and support as a human being, to let her know that here she can express her pain and that it will be accepted. Later I can ask her, How is it that your husband and your best friend chose each other to fall in love with? What part did you play in all of this? What are you getting from all this that is satisfactory to you? In order to help Lon with these questions I have no need to diagnose her, nor do I need to answer these questions theoretically.

Still later, should it prove useful to Lon, we can explore, if she is interested, how she feels about sex, what sex was like with her husband, what her own genital reactions are, her sex fantasies, what her pelvic movements are like, how enjoyable sex is, the quality of her orgasms, etc., etc. But only if it is useful to Lon. And still I do not need a diagnosis or a plan of therapy.

What about Beatrice, who feels betrayed? She was abandoned by her lover after five years of sharing a life. Here again I find little value in diagnosing Beatrice as a hostile, demanding, aggressive, phallic woman, ready to castrate her mate at the slightest provocation. Nor do I find it useful to think of Beatrice as a frightened, fantasy-ridden, narcissistic character disorder. Instead, I first want to assure her, despite this emotional blow to her vanity, that she is still a person of worth, deserving of respect. My plan, then, is to interrupt Beatrice from turning her hatred against herself, to help her gain some respect for herself and some distance from her immediate ache. Then when Beatrice is feeling more whole we can investigate what kind of relationship she had that could culminate in this type of abandonment. I can speculate on the relationship between her demandingness with me, her quickness to attack here, and what happened with her man. So far I need no diagnosis, just maintaining a closeness to Beatrice and where she is now.

Here you may ask if I am only soothing Beatrice. My response is that I am responding to Beatrice's needs at this moment. She feels abandoned and betrayed. So long as these feelings dominate her life, she will have little energy available to deal with how this came about, her own part in it. When she is feeling better about herself, then we can deal with more threatening matters. I am not trying to play the game of Truth with her, nor am I trying to force her to bite off more than she can digest at this moment. When she is ready, then I will ask her to look at larger segments of her life.

Should Beatrice begin to treat me as an authority who is asked to solve her problems, should she begin to complain of my attempts to judge her or control her, then I would probably find it useful to ask her where in the past she felt the same way. Perhaps with her absent man, perhaps with her father, perhaps with her mother. Yet I will be of greater use to Beatrice by staying close to what she reports, what she experiences here with me, than by trying to squeeze her into reproducing an Oedipal situation with me.

Gil is very guilty. He can't hold a job, a friend or a lover. He is perpetually in debt. I find it virtually useless to categorize him as a homosexual. When I talk to him I learn he is especially guilty about his choice of sexual partners. He feels worthless, doomed to a shabby life, hopelessly changing one job for another, one lover for another, and finding little fulfillment. I find it of small value to diagnose his schizoid detachment, his poor ability at forming deep interpersonal relationships. Instead, I want to interrupt Gil's misery by offering him hope. I do not try to support his restless quests, but instead I point out that he may be unsuccessful in changing his life until he first accepts himself right now. I might ask him to try not to make any changes at this moment but to stick with just what he is feeling, to get him to contact his self-loathing, to experience his sense of sin, to recognize how he is the architect of his dismal affairs, to take responsibility right now for the fact that his life is so unsatisfactory, that he is in debt. Now, what need have I for diagnosis at this point? Yet I am not so sure that I am willing to do away with the previous training I had, even though I might put it aside at any moment.

Bill tries to bully me. He is a talkative, aggressive man with a story to tell. He has prepared an autobiography and insists, though I show little interest, that he will recount his version, starting with early experiences. When I stop him to ask questions, he avoids answering. When I ask if he has noticed I do not share his enthusiasm for listening to his life, session after session, he continues to ignore me. When I ask him what he is leaving out that is not so well rehearsed, he becomes angry and sulks. He then asks how he can trust me, to tell him if the room is bugged, and then informs me, even if I assure him it is not bugged, that he in no way believes me.

Somehow through my clinical background and experience I

begin to wonder if I have a psychopath. And as soon as I begin thinking in diagnostic terms I know that something has happened to me. I have lost sympathy with Bill. I am no longer trying to reach him as a person but trying to reduce him to a thing, a category, a psychopath.

I reverse my tactics. I try to accept Bill at his own worth. But it is too late. He continues to talk at a rapid pace for a while. Then he slows down. He has decided that I am untrustworthy, that he cannot tell me what he thinks, what has happened to him. I think clinically in terms of paranoia and psychopathy, and soon it is all finished. He leaves therapy after only seven sessions, without calling to stop, without paying his bill. I can only comfort myself with a clinical diagnosis. And I am faced with my own limitation. Perhaps I cannot easily deal with psychopaths. Oh, well, his previous therapy lasted only one session.

Note, please, that in working with "Lon," "Beatrice," "Gil," "Bill" there are no miracle cures, no brilliant peak moments in which all is made clear and the person's problems are cracked open. I work in small steps, one at a time. Sometimes we walk backward, too, sometimes not in small steps. I can tell you that if you have been feeling better, stronger, more whole, and this has vanished at the moment, then it will return. In therapy, as in life (indeed, therapy is one part of life, not something apart from it), we (I include myself) move forward and backward.

By taking small steps I can feel comfortable; I do not lose you or myself. I lost Bill or recognized he was losing me when I took the leap of calling him a paranoid psychopath. I might not have been able to treat him anyway, but I would have had a better chance if I had stayed closer to him and what he was doing to me, how I felt about him, without needing to conceptualize his difficulties.

Taking small steps is hard work. It robs me of the opportunity to pull brilliant theories out of the air, to dazzle you with my expertise. I have to give up this kind of glamour unless I want to overwhelm you, to convince you that I am a magician, so that our relationship suffers, and you sit back and wait for me to work magic when you want it.

By taking small steps I ground myself much better in what is happening, and you are much better grounded. Then whatever new figures emerge in our work together we can both share excitement about. As the new figures develop, the better grounded we are with each other, the less we will need to retreat to a state of anxiety or tension. Together we have been building to this point so that together we can accept what is taking place now.

When I am most successful, in each session, we will discover new figures. We will find moments in which old patterns are suddenly illuminated and then drop away because their power fades with their exposure. Sometimes, though, we will have to settle for only catching glimpses or sensing forms that have not coalesced. Instead of a confusing blur we will have come to a vague outline, and I am pleased with that.

Karen vacillates between taking care of others and being helpless and taken care of. She is separated and has the custody of her four small children, with no child support. The pacifist group for which she works is having financial problems, and she has not been paid for three months. In one session I become very direct in my question. Who can you borrow from? Make a list. Who can you owe money to, who will extend you more credit? Make a list. Yet Karen resists being practical. So I attend to what is good about being broke. Make a case for living at the edge of poverty or even beyond it. Karen is quick to answer. She gets by in life by taking care of other people or having them take care of her. By staying with her poverty, she will elicit sympathy and someone will come through and bail her out. There is no need for me to formulate dependence; she has had years of therapy before and knows this. What I can offer Karen is a new experience of how she conspires to keep herself in need and the high price she is willing to pay for it.

She also points out that by being poor she can continue to

resent her ex-husband, to blackmail her parents, to feel so hectic and chaotic that she can avoid dealing with her own life, that she can construct a drama of herself as martyr, with a cruel world insensitive to her plight. Karen now has enough to chew over so that there is no need for me to make any interpretations or to offer any diagnoses.

At the next session she talks of her house, tells me that she spends more time there, locks the door and closes out the world. I ask her to be her house, to talk to me in the first person as her house.

Karen quickly tells me she feels big and strong, that she has thick walls. She goes on to report that she is filled with junk, that she is chaotic and disorderly. I ask her to tell me about the junk, and she responds that there is a furnace that has exploded, cobwebs and old paint cans. I ask her to be the exploded furnace, the cobwebs and the old paint cans. She tells me as the furnace that she is worthless, just takes up space, was once in good condition, but after she blew up she has never been repaired. As a cobweb she tells me that she can't survive any active, lively movement, that she is fragile and crumbles on contact with others. As old paint Karen informs me that she is stiff and congealed, that her colors have separated and lost their coherence.

I do not press Karen for false solutions to her need for a spring cleanup. I am satisfied if she can contact her despair and feel how out of sorts her life is. At the same time, by being able to express her messiness, by not avoiding or denying it, Karen feels relief and that precious commodity, hope.

Note once again that in working with Karen I have no need to conceptualize what is happening between us in any theoretical terms. I could talk about the defensive mechanisms of denial and projection, but what would I be doing with my contact with Karen while I was engaging in this dialogue?

Yet I confess that I live a double life as a therapist. On the one hand my training with Laura and Isadore permits me to stay with each person, attending to what is happening between us. On the other hand my academic training and my analytic experience are not erased. I use psychoanalytic theory and academic training as a foundation from which I ground myself. I can only be myself in the therapeutic encounter, and since I possess both backgrounds, I try to use them so that they blend together rather than clash. Thus, while I am working I try to feel and experience what is happening between us at the same time I go off (the deep end?) and try to use my intellectual background for whatever it is worth to inform me further as to what is happening. I trust what I feel more, but I also keep informed of what my head is telling me in terms of some clinical background. However, I try to keep this clinical knowledge as background. At times I deliberately make myself dumb so that I can experience anew, freshly, what is happening between us, so that I don't in a stale way pick out of my store of information the "correct" answer as to what is happening, the "right" way of proceeding to deal with the situation in front of me. Similarly, at times I will neglect a "tried and true" method that I know works well, to invent on the spur of the moment a new way of dealing with what is happening in front of me. The challenge I invent helps also to keep me alive and fresh rather than detached and stereotyped in my response. You see, I too must *be there*, with you, if our transaction is to be vivid.

When you feel vivid and alive, excited and tingling, then you are in a different place, able to deal with your own perceptions, thoughts, feelings in a more vital way with which you can connect. One of the goals of Gestalt Therapy is within each session to find means of making your experience vivid and exciting. If you can connect, right now, in a lively, excited way with what is happening in your life, then you cannot be stuck, blocked, at an impasse.

At the same time, if you are stuck at an impasse, unable to get beyond being stuck, then I would ask you to accept this right now as who you are. To accept that at this point you are still getting too much out of your conflict to deal with it. Here once again, by accepting this impasse as a part of yourself, without blame, you have changed how you look at yourself, so that you cannot go on with the stereotyped picture of yourself as someone to blame. Then here, too, we have changed your picture of yourself. And this is also one of the aims of Gestalt Therapy, to try new means of looking at yourself, to see if there is some new way of finding out how you deal with the world, to try to accept where you are now in its fullest meaning, to make even this experience of your being stuck a vivid, lively picture.

Now a clever reader will ask, It's true that you do not appear to have the same need to diagnose a person in order to work with him in therapy; yet obviously this does not establish that you are working within an atheoretical framework. How do you decide in what manner to proceed? And if the reader is attentive, he will recognize that my principle is related to what is happening here and now with the person as I work with him.

To be somewhat more precise, as I work my primary focus is not on the past or on a need for a diagnosis or a theory but to attend to what is happening right now in front of me. Thus, you can get me to confess that I work from the principle of *immediacy*, in which what is happening right now or is felt so vividly right now is not experienced as a part of a distant past but as a living present, a throbbing current unfinished situation.

Now the reader will at this point question me further with the thought, Well, so much is happening right now, how do you decide which part of the overwhelming, booming present to focus on? And here the answer stems directly from the principles of Gestalt formation. While I attend to any event or activity, I am actively sorting it out to try to make some kind of sense out of it. That which is of little interest, of no concern, I permit to recede to the background, and I concentrate on the foreground. So when I am hungry I attend primarily to the food and not the plate. And in such an obvious example there is no conflict as to what is foreground and what is background. On the other hand, should I be hungry and attend to the plate and not the food, that would be an unusual event that would draw my interest to discovering why this is happening.

Here, again, the reader will note that I must have some implicit sense of order that dictates that when eating it is preferable to pay attention to the food and not the plate. Now here I must be careful in answering that to be a good Gestalt therapist I have to avoid my own implicit biases and question them. When would it make sense, even if hungry, to attend to the plate rather than the food? Possible answers: if I have such a highly developed aesthetic sense that the presentation of food is sometimes more important than the food itself; if I am in a tropical country where sanitary conditions are not too rigorous, and I want to assure myself that the plate is reasonably clean; if I am a rigid person frightened of germs who needs to inspect all his food before he can eat it.

In other words, if I am really to be in touch with what is happening, I need to have a sense of what is usual and unusual as well as an ability to be flexible, to be alert to what other possibilities are at hand but do not yet figure for me. I need to reverse the usual figure-ground formation so that I have a greater awareness of what is happening right now.

Once again the careful reader will return and ask again, I understand what you are saying about the importance of the immediate situation. I see what you mean by the need to pay attention to the obvious foreground and then to be flexible enough to make it background, but I am still at a loss to know how you decide in an actual situation how to respond with a particular person, what to select to begin with. For example, suppose someone comes to see you. When he arrives he slumps in, barely breathing, falls onto a chair. His face is drawn and his eyes are glazed. What do you say? Why, you have made it too easy. Obviously the person is in distress. I say nothing. I give him a chance to collect himself, and when he has he will begin to *orient* me as to what is important. You see, I need to orient myself as to who I am with each time. I cannot assume that who I saw last week is the same person who is with me now. I have no way of knowing what has happened during the week. I try not to have a fixed figure, a rigid Gestalt of who I am with, of what has happened between us in the past, so that I don't get stuck with what was rather than dealing with what is.

Yes, yes, you reply, somewhat impatiently, I understand your points about the need for a flexible, lively, current Gestalt, but you have not answered my question. I begin to suffer from this unfinished piece of business from the past. Tell me, if you will or can, how you select from among the vast range of figures which one you will attend to in working with a person.

I reply, Now I understand your need for closure. You do indeed have a piece of unfinished business from your past that is interfering right now with your ability to understand me. I suspect that what you are unaware of is that you want me to offer you some "right" way of working as a therapist. You want to find out what the rules are so that you can understand what is a "good" therapist. Now let me give you two answers.

First, there is no "right" way of selecting what to attend to. You can only rely on yourself. Suppose I use as my rule that it is always best to wait for the other to begin the session, to see what is foreground for him. Yet suppose in the situation I mentioned earlier (a harassed man enters and sinks into a chair) you offer a human response such as, You look very upset. Why, this may elicit a rush of feeling of being cared for, and this might be more useful therapeutically than a long recital of what caused the distress. How is anyone to know then what is right? You cannot. I repeat, you can only learn to trust yourself and your experience.

Now I will give you the second answer I promised, and perhaps that will satisfy you. When I am perplexed as to what is important, I have a number of questions I can ask myself or the person with whom I am working. I can ask myself, What can I do that will offer more contact at this moment? I can ask such questions as what are you feeling right now, what would you like to talk about, what are you thinking about but not talking about? Or I can take my own observation as a point of making contact. You look very upset right now. Are you losing weight? Just now as you walked across the room I was struck by how you hold your hips when you move. Can you describe this for me? Are you aware of how you do it?

Perhaps if I am less anxious about being such a good therapist and always doing the right thing, then I can also have some confidence that if at times I begin by making a mistake, then if I am relaxed, I can recover from my error; I can drop a fruitless approach and go on. Now in order to know that I have a fruitless line of inquiry I will have to be in contact with what has emerged from my experience right now. So once again I attend to what is happening right now, here, between us, and this informs me how to proceed. I repeat: If I make an error, then it can be corrected. There is no disaster. I can make errors, unless I need to be an omnipotent therapist, always right, always in touch. If this were so, then I would have to attend to my own vanity and perfectionism and note how my attention is directed away from you and your needs and toward my own need to be perfect and important.

Aha. Now you do not find such urgency in getting me to answer how I would select from all that is there. Perhaps, then, it is a good moment to pause.

3 . My Work

What is it that I do? How can I describe my work? I look and listen, that's for sure. I look as hard as I can, try to see as much as I can, and sometimes my eyes ache from it. I try to see with my eyes everything I can about how you sit, how you walk, how you breathe, how you avoid looking at me, how you hesitate before saying a thought you don't like, how you tense the parts of your body, how you hold your mouth, your neck. I look at the clothes you wear, their style or lack of it, how neat, clean or dirty. I look at your face above all; I try to read the emotions on your face. If necessary I confess to trying to read your mind by looking into your head through your eyes.

And I listen. I listen and listen. And as I listen I think. I look for patterns of thought, for ideas I can bring together. I listen for emotions, feelings that are hidden or disconnected, misplaced or forgotten. I try to bring these feelings into the open, to make them clear and sparkling. I try to take your thoughts and to assemble them so that you can see them in a fresh way that is not just one after the other but side by side or interacting with one another so that you can make something new out of them.

But although I am already feeling better about what I do, I realize that this is not enough. We have something to do together, and this is what is most vital.

I must struggle with your demons and still leave you more, not less, for their being slain. I need to let you know that I care, in some instances more than you do. I need to reassure you that I take some aspects of your life more seriously than you. And then when you feel secure that you don't have to take care of yourself, that I care enough to do it for you, why, then I have to pull the rug out from under you and remind you that after all, much as I care, it is really your own life, and I may care, but you will have to take care of yourself; I have no intention of doing that for you.

I have to be particularly nimble in this area of struggling with your demon. You have spent a lifetime developing means of trapping yourself and anyone else who tries to deal with you. I try not to become conceited, to assume that I know all the patterns you can invent to trick or trap me. Half of the fun of my job is to remain fresh so that I can learn something new all the time, because if I am really clear and honest enough, then I can invent a new kind of therapy not only for each person but for each session.

In order to be able to do this even remotely I have to be willing to be there, not just for you but for me as well. I have to be willing to examine whatever is happening in front of me and not assimilate it too quickly to a stale model. I have to try to be flexible enough to form a different relationship with each person, to be willing to be alive enough to differences and to take risks in not needing to tell myself I know everything that is going on.

In order to be fresh I need to be able to forget what I have learned and to invent it for myself right now before you, so that it is tailored to you, so that we both feel it to be alive and vital. I have to risk forgetting what I know and then not being able to recall it. I have to risk that in making myself so innocent I will miss what my experience should have taught me. I have to risk not holding back, plunging ahead and making mistakes. I have to be willing to admit my mistakes and be wrong. Yet it is worth taking these risks, because I am gambling for your life, and my confidence comes from the belief that if I risk myself so openly, if I dare confront you in the ways that others avoid or that you ignore, I am betting that you will respond, that something can and will happen between us.

So I don't just look and listen; I talk a lot. I am constantly letting you know what I am receiving, what I am thinking, what I am feeling. And here again is another burden, somehow to remain fresh enough so that I can continue to feel, so that I don't become numb or overwhelmed or intimidated or cynical. Oh, yes, I know all too well those feelings I just enumerated, but I need to believe in myself enough so that when I begin to feel bored or numb, intimidated or overwhelmed, I can not only accept their validity but also ask you if there is not an important connection between what I am feeling and what you are also feeling, what you are doing to help stimulate me in this fashion. I believe that all this attention must flatter you, that you must respond to my interest in little old you. You always suspected you were interesting in some way, but here you have my complete attention. And so I sit. And as I grow older in this work of mine, sitting becomes more of a difficulty. I get stiff, my body rebels, my mind is not so sharp, and if I must sit for so many hours a day, then I must also find ways of relieving the tedium of sitting for so long. I have to find means of exercising so that I can be alert and fresh. I have to find ways of pacing myself so that after one session I am not spent emotionally, so that I won't be pressed to present a phony kind of eagerness and interest. Sometimes when I do become spent, when your suffering takes me over, then I confess to others that I am drained, and I will try to do the best I can.

Yes, your demons are always there, always testing me, always trying to outwit me. And so as I listen to you, as I look at you, as I listen to myself and try to feel myself, so I am often trying to guess what new form the demon will take and how I can outwit him before he outwits me. All of this makes for lively interaction, and if it weren't, then how could I survive the strain? Somehow I enjoy the struggle, our encounter, our confrontation. Sometimes you are too stubborn, and I become weary, the battle palls. I can take a lot of failure, especially if I feel that waiting at the end of it your demon will also tire, be lulled offguard, feel overly confident, think that I am a pushover. But if I feel pushed beyond what I can endure, then I become cross and let you know that I am reaching my own limits. If we are to find some way of making this thing work, of getting together, then I need some kind of assurance for myself. Yes, I accept the challenge. I will take on you and your demon. And I am serious. I will try to find a new way of reaching out to him, a special tailored means of getting to treat your special condition. Each session will be different, each encounter will be unique. Unless, of course, you severely restrict my ability to contact you. And then my own means become limited. If you don't come, or if you come but refuse to talk to me, then I have less movement in which to respond to you. I still have a range of choices, but after I have exhausted them—for there is only a relatively narrow range of how I can respond to absence or silence—then I will have to repeat myself in some kind of variation. So your minimal cooperation is one of the best ways of seeing that both you and your demon survive intact.

When I listen I have to pay particular attention to your use of words. We may think that language was developed as a means of communication, but we are all so clever that as we use language with more facility it also becomes a means of not communicating. I have to develop the means of hearing what you are saying and then of hearing what you are not saying, of letting your words come through and then stopping and questioning you closely about a particular word, a particular usage, a phrase. I try not to race ahead and tell myself what you mean by your special meanings, for then I become invested in proving myself right, smart, clever. But occasionally, if I am feeling very relaxed, I will permit myself this kind of lapse and let you in on it too.

Am I honestly serious when I say that I want to invent a new psychotherapy for each person? I try to be, to have a fresh approach for each of you. And at the same time I have the obligation to myself to be recognizably me, someone who is not play-acting. Sometimes this puts a strain on me, and I will try to point out where and how I manage it.

Gerald. He lies almost all the time. He withholds information. He distorts. I see him in a group, so I inadvertently get reports from others in the group, but I also know from his own reports that it is not only a matter of not being able to face the truth but a deliberate attempt to manipulate others either through his outright lies or through withholding information that is vital.

In my previous life as a historian I was passionately involved in the search for the truth. All my sources had to be double-checked, all my references pure, all my data achingly checked for accuracy, my interpretations severely limited by the laws of logic and inference, tied to my materials. And now I sit and listen to lies and distortions. My gorge riseth, but I am not there to sit and check accuracy or, as Paul Lazarsfeld reported to Edward Suchman (two well-known sociologists), "We are not boy scouts." So, although I choke when I hear the lies, I have something more important on my mind than the prosecuting-attorney role, attempting to nail down the truth, just give me the facts. I am after something greater than the truth, the intention of building a relationship with Gerald, so that on his own, of his own free will, he will come to the use of the truth as a preferable mode of dealing with others. On his own. At this point he still feels threatened by others so that lies are part of his security system. They occur in fewer numbers, they are open to self-corrections, but they still occur.

So I resist the urge to play the scholar-pedant-attorney, looking for accuracy and truth. And this costs me a great deal; it makes our sessions more painful for me. I have to spend time with myself, reminding me that I am not there primarily for my own purposes but for his.

When we first began we were far away from any question of lies or distortions. Language was used by Gerald in such a private manner that I had all I could do to hang in, to try to determine what he was trying to say, never mind if it was true or not. He had already seen more than half a dozen therapists before me, so he had lots of time to develop techniques for talking and not being understood, being there and not being there, pretending to look for help and then making help impossible. I must confess that at times I became dizzy. What was he trying to say? Why was it being said in this way, in code as it were? I had accepted that our time together would be long and that I would have to be very patient. I was not looking for miracle cures. I was not sure how far we could go together. Many others had failed, and why should I be different?

Well, over the years the changes have occurred, and I have outlasted the other therapists. Yes, I am proud of it, and I think I know why some of this has happened. My patience and acceptance of Gerald as he wanted to present himself has surely been a great help. I took his side, listened to him, asked questions that were as little threatening as possible, tried to nudge him toward looking at other interpretations of events he was involved in, did not question his veracity and slowly gained his grudging belief that I did not want to harm him. Yet every time I pushed for greater independence, responsibility, manliness on his part, he became angry, attacked, withdrew, renewed his distrust which was always there, at best minimally in check. I talked about distrust, but we got no further most of the time than yes, mistrust was certainly there, but I would have to put up with it. When I suggested that he did not have to put up with it he became angry, he was satisfied, he wanted to continue. We had great battles on occasion, particularly when I refused to go along with all of his demands. I was clear that I had my limits and beyond these I would not go. He was angry, protested, threatened, cried, cursed and in the end was grateful that I was steadfast.

Gradually during this period Gerald's opinion of himself changed. He originally justified his stance toward others in his life because he saw himself as helpless, rejected, deprived. He was angry, envious, needy, grasping. In our work together and in group he came to see that he was not helpless but powerful, much more powerful than he had dared to hope. He learned that he was not so much rejected as rejecting, sometimes brutally attacking others. If he had been deprived in the past, then in the present he had a great deal more than others. I particularly tried to point out how we could make a case for reversing positions, how I might envy him and myself feel deprived vis-a-vis him. He laughed and said he preferred not to accept this, but later he could quote accurately all the points I had made. As he learned that he could take care of his own needs or that others were quite willing in many, though not all, ways to supply him, he became less anxious and threatened. He reluctantly began to have a better view of himself and widened his transactions with the world. And through it all I tried to be there for him, tried not to judge or, if I had to make a judgment, to be clear that my judgment was coming from my own need to make judgments rather than as a truth.

Gerald began to copy me in various ways. He took parts that he felt were useful and appropriated them as his own. My fear was that he would simply swallow what was easy, but no, he worked at what he took so that he wears much of it gracefully and is effective in his own version. He can still shed this new acquisition rapidly and return to being needy, but now he has more strings to his bow than he had before.

I now feel able to raise the issue of truth, and we can talk about openness in relationships. But the issue is not a matter of truth. When Gerald feels strong and able, when he feels confident and responsible, then the truth is fairly easy to put forth. When he feels threatened in some of the ways that are still unresolved, then the lies and distortions blossom. With time, though, these areas of threat have been reduced, and who knows but with more time and patience his need for this type of control will become even smaller. He may never end up as the scholar-pedant I admire from my graduate-student days in history, but he will be able to have relationships that are rewarding for him and for those around him. I no longer feel the same strains myself. Now we share a common language and an ability to talk to each other and be understood. And along with this has come a halting affection and an acceptance on his part. This means I can be less patient and more demanding myself. My patience has paid off, and now I can use other tactics. We continue to grow and develop our relationship.

Helen. She has spent most of her life in psychotherapy or psychoanalysis. She is very bright and very shrewd. She has so many ways of trapping me. I enjoy our sessions, even though I realize that although I go along with where she is leading me, I will suddenly find that I am somewhere else and I have committed a grievous therapeutic fault. Sometimes Helen tries to provoke me into attacking her so that she can feel wounded and withdraw in righteous hatred; other times she tries to get me to attack her so that she can feel justified in her own self-hatred. Then there are the times that she traps me so that she can be justified in hating me for my stupidity.

During the early first sessions she made witty and humorous remarks about herself in a friendly, open, self-deprecating manner. When I equally openly laughed, enjoying her wit and sarcasm, she attacked me for joining in and laughing at her sad condition, for being taken in by her attempts to use humor to cover her sadness. I pointed out my trap. If I didn't laugh, I was being too serious, refusing to participate in a situation she was taking pains to construct; I was playing the stuffy therapist who controlled all lightness and play, when she was openly inviting me to laugh. If I did laugh, then I was an insensitive fool, enjoying myself at her expense. I began to learn that the rules were being constructed so that I could not win, no matter what I did.

Helen complained that she had expressly sought me out because she wanted Gestalt Therapy; she did not want talk therapy. She was sick of words and ideas. She wanted to vomit because she was so tired of all this talk, and nothing else happened. I felt I was on the spot, and although I did not feel experiments were called for, I offered to comply with her request-demands. She promptly fell silent and refused to comply. How could she do these crazy things? She was blocked. What good could come out of this? There, you see now she had done it, and all she felt was humiliation and degradation. Obviously I had failed again. I had tried to go along with her own idea of what she wanted, and the result was Helen in tears, blaming herself, feeling cheated, crying that there was no hope.

Helen said she wanted greater personal contact, wanted to know about my life, who I was, how I felt. She was tired of the anonymity of the therapist. I complied and tried to answer her questions. Then she turned on me and complained, Why did I inject myself so much in the therapy? Why did I talk so much? She really was there for herself and not to hear about my life.

Sometimes I felt hurt and attacked, but gradually I discovered that by going along with Helen's requests it didn't make much difference what she asked for; either she had to feel bad or evil, or she had to feel that I was bad or evil and that she was good. Now that was something worth finding out, even if it meant being trapped over and over again. Once I learned this, I could easily submit to her traps but point out to her what was happening. I no longer had to watch my own steps so closely, for I knew that no matter what I did I would end up cast as a villain or a hero. I tried to avoid falling into the traps easily, but Helen was smart enough, and there were endless variations. What was important was that she not only became aware of her trapping herself and others but also she was grateful for my own willingness to submit to her traps without making her pay a price or without having to pay a price myself.

Helen is unmarried and wants a husband and children. She also feels extremely sensitive to any discussion on these topics. We have developed a routine for talking about sex, men, masturbation, dating. She tells me, and I would like to believe her, that during her five years of psychoanalysis she never was able to talk about men or sex, so she just lied about it. When either she or I agree to talk about sex, Helen becomes very defensive. She feels attacked, no matter what is said. She then attacks either me or herself. I am familiar enough with the process by now that I can just let her go on. Soon she will cry, and then she will be able to calm down and look at what we have been talking about without all the heat and terror. After two years we can now talk easily about sex and men. Even about Helen's feelings for her father.

At first I was concerned with Helen's tears and wanted to help her stop crying so much. But she would have none of it. Her tears were part of her view of her life as being full of pain. If I didn't like them, then that was too bad. As I got to know her better I also learned that she feels she has a rock inside her and that this rock weighs her down. When she cries the rock becomes lighter. She melts a little in terms of her harsh attitudes toward herself, and her tears help express her loosening up.

Often when Helen is angry she withdraws. However, her withdrawal is not just a simple form of pouting. In order to avoid her guilt over her anger, she breaks contact and then her withdrawal is massive. She begins to think that I am angry with her and that she ought to leave therapy. She decides she will arrive for the last time, and once there, since it is the last session and since things are hopeless, she might as well just sit and say nothing. My job is somehow to find a means of permitting Helen to recognize her anger toward me without being immobilized by her guilt. If she were not an unusually appealing person, I might be prepared to let her quit and be done with it. Even so I feel sorely tried. Her anger is quickly covered by guilt or spite. That is fair enough; the textbooks are filled with such examples. But it is the intensity with which Helen attacks herself or me that is different. Her face is screwed into a hateful leer, her fingers claw the air with disgust, her voice rasps. My only hope is to get Helen to see how much fun she is getting out of the whole thing or to make her laugh. For now we are good enough friends that I can accept her misery without being sucked into it. And by having paid my dues by first permitting her to suck me into her misery, I can now get her to quit the club by staying outside and asking her to join me there.

I am asking a lot. Helen has spent most of her adult life, and a good deal of her childhood, manipulating her world so that she can have the safety of being rejected or rejecting others. She makes friends now, but she is aware that she is half pretending. First she will be good and woo her friend, but she will collect a series of wrongs and when she feels resentful or guilty enough, then she will attack her new friend. But the attack will not be something that will make the new friend just unhappy. Helen's attack is intended to devastate, to annihilate the new friend.

I am not the most patient of men, so if I am to work with Helen I must also work on myself. I have to learn to expand my range of patience, I have to learn to be able to submit to traps and not feel vulnerable, I have to be able to bear her powerful anger directed against me, I have to learn not to be torn apart by her own misery. So by staying with Helen I have to grow myself. I like to believe I become a better therapist by Helen's teaching me, and by my being honest with Helen about her contribution to me she is more willing to trust me and to believe that I am honestly interested in her well-being.

So we lurch from crisis to crisis. From my point of view, the crises become less intense and are wider-spaced. Her professional life is more secure; she has a better social life. She still is unsure of herself with regard to men, but she has now widened her range of friends to include men—a new departure. What happens next we will see in the next session. And then the one after that . . .

4 . A Sample Session

Here is a session with Harold that recapitulates a lot of the material we had been going over for more than a year. I felt free to summarize a lot because we had gone over a great deal of it in different contexts several times.

HAROLD: In the group the other day I opened with Terry and told him that I wanted to be his friend, and we hugged. Then I called him later in the week and went over to see him and Jeanette. I had a lousy time. I felt like I didn't want to be there, I just wanted to be by myself. Then I couldn't leave. I stayed long after I wanted to. I was so mad at myself. I was feeling so crummy.

ME: Were you feeling awkward or clumsy when you went to see Terry?

HAROLD: Yes, yes. I *was* feeling clumsy. (*Smiles with pleasure.*)

ME: (*Lecture. Information.*): Whenever we begin something new or strange we are apt to feel awkward or clumsy. Can you remember when you first started therapy how difficult it was for you to come and talk with me? And until you got over your awkwardness, this was a barrier to your becoming more open, closer. And can you remember when you first had the idea of starting to approach Linda how frightened you felt, how you had no right to approach her and how clumsy you felt about asking her for a date?

Harold nods.

39

ME: If you want to develop anything new, you will have to endure your own lack of skill at the beginning. You will have to risk being awkward or clumsy or embarrassed (*end of lecture*). What would be good about being clumsy and holding on to it?

HAROLD: I could stick to my own feelings and ignore what was going on outside of me. I could feel so uncomfortable that I could decide it wasn't worth going on with the whole thing, and then withdraw. But I didn't expect any of that.

ME: What did you expect?

HAROLD: I thought that after that experience in group everything would be easy. I thought that now Terry and I were going to be friends.

ME: Were going to be friends?

HAROLD: Yes. I thought now that I hugged him, I *have* to feel close to him. And instead I feel embarrassed.

ME: You have to feel close to him? Where did you get that idea?

HAROLD (*shrugs*): I don't know. I just have it.

ME: Well, it must have come from somewhere.

HAROLD: I don't know.

ME: Who says if you hug Terry once that you *have* to be his friend?

HAROLD: I guess I do.

ME: Can you remember when you first started sleeping with Linda you had the idea that you had to be in love with her if you had sex with her? Can you remember that you felt at that time if you slept with her that you had to want to see her when she wanted to see you and that when you wanted to leave you didn't have the right?

HAROLD: Yes, I can remember that now, but I forget those things.

ME: But you can remember that more easily now. Can you see here that you tend to make up rules about how things have to be and then feel overwhelmed?

HAROLD: I don't know that I am doing it at the time. I just feel that things have to be this way.

ME: And then you get resentful and rebellious at the rules you have to submit to. But who has created them?

HAROLD (*silence*): I know I have, but I don't know I am doing it at the time that I am doing them.

ME: I think what you do is that first you have a feeling—I want to be close to Terry, I want to sleep with Linda—and then you start to *think* about it and make up all sorts of rules. If I want to be Terry's friend, then I *ought* to like him *all* the time, I *ought* to feel close to him all the time. If I want to sleep with Linda, then I *should* fall in love with her, I *should* want to see her all the time, I should want to please her. Naturally, you get resentful with these burdens, and you feel guilty when you can't live up to the demands you have created.

HAROLD (*with great exasperation*): Why do I do this all the time? (*pause*) I know I don't have to, but I keep forgetting.

ME: How is it that you forget so easily what you have learned with so much difficulty?

HAROLD: I don't know. I just don't think.

ME: I think what you do is avoid thinking and feeling. You *ought* to love Linda is a stale idea whose time belongs to the past. You *ought* to be Terry's best friend and love him all the time is another. When you avoid letting yourself know what you are feeling, are thinking, when instead you settle for listening to old, stale records of what should be happening, you get stuck.

HAROLD: I am stuck!

ME: I know that when I am not feeling good I get stuck. In my own past it was easy for me to ignore machines and tools. It's still easy for me to do that, but if I make the effort, I can learn and feel better about who I am. In your case, it was easy to know about machines and tools but not about feelings. When you take the time to stay with your feelings, then you feel stronger, better about yourself, in charge of what is happening in your life.

HAROLD: You're right! I don't think. I won't feel. It seems like so much effort.

ME: And then what happens?

HAROLD: Then I feel oppressed by what I ought to do, by what is expected of me. And then I get resentful. Fuck you! You're not going to tell me what to do! And so I do nothing.

ME: Let me try to clarify. First you ignore your own feelings and instead substitute old thoughts. Then you get resentful and withdrawn. What you have done is to leave your own experience and substitute a script. What you seem unaware of is that the script continues, so that you can end by withdrawing from Linda or Terry because of their supposed demands, and you can feel justified. There you are, righteous and lonely. Now how do you feel?

HAROLD: Guilty! Guilty! Guilty! I feel guilty if I don't live up to what Linda expects of me, and I feel guilty if I avoid her because I don't want to live up to her demands, or the demands which I pretend she feels.

ME: And whenever you feel guilty, you want to blame someone else.

HAROLD: I know all this, but what can I do? We have been over it so many times.

ME: It doesn't matter how many times we go over it. The important thing is for you to see what you are doing to yourself and others. You still leave your feelings. And now if you don't feel free to blame Terry or Linda for your own thoughts, then you want to get me to blame you. You're determined to feel guilty, one way or another.

HAROLD: But won't it ever end? How do I ever get rid of my guilt?

ME: What are you doing now, in this whole session?

HAROLD: I—I'm feeling helpless and asking you to give me all the answers.

ME: And I have probably been giving you too many of them. Shall I join you in feeling guilty? Shall I join you by making you feel more guilty? What do you want from me?

HAROLD: Sure I want you to give me the answers. That's easier.

ME: Maybe that's why you get so little out of some of these sessions. It's too easy. You ask questions and kind old Dan gives answers. He feels good and you feel good, and nothing happens. How is that? Maybe you don't do much with the answers he gives, and then you can feel guilty for not listening to him when he was nice enough to answer your questions.

HAROLD: Well, I asked you what I could do.

ME: Be aware of what you are doing. Playing helpless. Looking for someone else to do your work. Avoiding thinking about what you set up. I admit I cooperate too easily. Avoiding thinking about what happens, about what you feel. Rushing forward to feel guilty at the slightest provocation. What is so good about being guilty so much of the time?

HAROLD: Well, if you're guilty, then it means you wanted to do better. It means no one else can blame you for what you didn't do if you blame yourself first. It means that you should be perfect and you can apologize in advance for not being perfect. It means you can avoid what you want to and just pay for it a little bit by feeling guilty.

ME: So you get a lot out of feeling guilty.

HAROLD: Oh, yes. I've been guilty for a long time. I know it well.

ME: I hope you can stay in touch with how much you get out of it. Suppose you could do all of those things you want to without feeling guilty. I think you mentioned not being blamed, not having to be perfect, not having to apologize in advance, not having to avoid what you want to.

HAROLD: How could I do that?

ME: How about taking responsibility for yourself? Then you don't have to blame yourself. I wanted to do this. I wanted to do that. I didn't want to do this. I didn't want to do that.

HAROLD: Wow! I'm not sure. I don't think I am ready for that yet.

ME: So you are fairly comfortable with your guilt and prefer it to being responsible.

HAROLD: I guess so. But I never knew it in this way. I may want to be responsible for myself. But at this moment, that seems too frightening. If it's O.K. with you, I think I want to just stick with trying to see when I am going on a guilt trip, and let it go at that.

ME: O.K. with me? Are you trying to make me responsible right now for you? I won't do it. You can decide for yourself. If you decide not to be responsible now, will you feel guilty?

HAROLD: No. I think if I can be responsible for knowing when I prefer to be guilty, when I make a choice to be guilty, then I don't have to be guilty for doing it. Oh, what am I saying! If I *choose* to be guilty, then I can be guilty without having to be guilty about my choice. Does that make sense?

ME: It does to me.

HAROLD: There's something else I want to talk about. When I think about getting close to Terry, I get excited. No, I don't mean sexually. I think I know enough about my homosexual feelings not to be nervous about that. But at the same time I get excited. I get frightened. What will happen next? I get worried. I think he will get too close to me.

ME: Too close?

HAROLD: Yes. I feel afraid of closeness. That if he gets close, and we become good friends, then he will take me over.

ME: Take you over?

HAROLD: Well, not exactly take me over. I don't know. I think he'll want all these things from me, and I'll have to give them to him. I think I won't be able to do what I want.

ME: Why not?

HAROLD: I think that if I don't do exactly what he wants, then he'll get angry and stop being my friend.

ME: Are you saying that to be friends you have to submit to Terry's wishes and ignore your own?

HAROLD: I guess that's what I'm saying, but when I hear it it doesn't make much sense.

ME: Can you try to tell me what you are afraid of?

HAROLD: Well, it's not a power trip. I'm not afraid of being dominated by Terry.

ME: Are you sure?

HAROLD: No. As a matter of fact, I'm not so sure. I think I can take care of myself, but when I get close I get confused. I'm not sure of what I feel.

ME: What are you confused about?

HAROLD: Let's see. I get confused because I don't know what's right. I get confused because I'm not sure where he is and where I am.

ME: Are you looking for rules again for what's right?

HAROLD: Yeah. I guess so.

ME: What is right in friendship?

HAROLD: Whatever we both agree to, whatever we both like, I guess.

ME: You guess?

HAROLD: All right. I'm trying to avoid facing it. We can both decide in what way we can be friends.

ME: But you sound so angry when you say that. Why?

HAROLD: Because I really feel, deep down, that there is a right way to be friends, no matter what I may know with my head, that there is one right way to do things.

ME: Then tell me the right way to do things.

HAROLD: You have to—

ME: *You* have to? Do you mean *you* or *I?*

HAROLD: You have to—

ME: But can you see that if *you* have to, *I* don't have to?

HAROLD: No. I really can't see that. We all have to do the same thing. That's what I feel. I can't help it. I know it doesn't make any sense, but that's how I feel.

ME: Then let yourself feel that. Feel right now how you have one idea of how a friendship ought to be and then try to feel what happens if Terry has another idea of how friendship ought to be.

HAROLD: Then we'll fight, of course. And whoever is stronger will dominate the weaker.

ME: And that's what you call friendship? No wonder you have so much trouble getting closer to Terry.

HAROLD: No. That's not what I call friendship. I can frighten myself into getting lost in the power trip. But I honestly think I'm more frightened of feeling close to him. I can feel O.K. about fighting with him as a friend. That's easier than feeling close to him.

ME: Try to imagine that he's here now. That you are feeling close to him and he is feeling close to you.

HAROLD: I feel I'm going to disappear. That he's going to swallow me. That he has to take me over. Not because of the power trip but just that I can't be close without disappearing.

ME: How do you feel about that, about being taken over?

HAROLD: I feel very frightened, very small.

ME: Now could you try to see if you could in your imagination let yourself go along with being taken over, could you see what it is like to be swallowed by Terry?

HAROLD (pause): I don't feel so bad. I kind of like it. I feel warm and protected and not frightened. It's sort of nice. (pause) But now I'm beginning to get a little bored.

ME: Could you let yourself separate from Terry now, after you have been taken over?

HAROLD: Sure. That feels better. Now I'm outside of him.

ME: How do you feel?

HAROLD: I feel fine. I liked being swallowed, and then I got bored. And I feel better for letting myself do the whole thing.

ME: Now how do you feel about getting close to Terry?

HAROLD: I don't feel so frightened about getting close. I guess if I want to, I can get close and even taken over and enjoy that. And if I'm not enjoying it, I guess I can stop it.

ME: You guess?

HAROLD: O.K., O.K. I don't have to be closer than I want.

ME: Are you saying that to please me, because it is the "right" answer?

HAROLD: I don't know.

ME: Who can I ask?

HAROLD (with anger): O.K. So I don't want to know.

ME: If it's O.K. with you, it's O.K. with me. It's your life, not mine. And you can live it as you please.

HAROLD: I don't like it, but I do get tired of having to be responsible all the time.

ME: And yet you won't let Terry or Linda or me take over. You end up being unhappy no matter what happens. Unhappy, guilty, resentful. Maybe that's a good way to stop—with your feeling those things.

HAROLD: But I don't want to.

ME: I'm not so sure. Try to look at how much you get out of being stuck there, and if *you* want to we can talk about it again.

5 . Fail and Farewell

It's not working out. We are both dissatisfied. I know why I am because I have had a lot of experience, because it's part of my job to be aware of what is happening and not happening between us and how I respond to it. I try to talk to you about the fact that you come late to sessions repeatedly, that when I point this out you aren't particularly interested, that sometimes you don't show up at all, don't even call to let me know. I point this out and wonder if you are trying to provoke me, but you still feign a lack of interest. Then I find I do begin to get angry. I explain how I feel about this, that instead of a partnership in which we both meet for our mutual purposes, you are turning it into something that suits you on a whimsical basis.

I ask you how we can proceed, what you intend to do about being late, how you feel about what I have just said. You still plead indifference, then become slightly angry at being pushed by me to do something that is beyond your control. You can't help it if you are late; it is a part of your nature; you have always been late; you were born late, a week overdue; the labor itself lasted seventeen hours. Late again. I point out that you are saying you are helpless, that this is beyond your control, but when you go to the theater or a movie you want to see you get there on time; that when you were a student you got to class on time, but now you suddenly claim that what we have agreed to is beyond your ability. I now feel less angry and more skeptical.

I ask once more what can we arrange, granted my needs. You

protest that I am not fair, that I am just like your parents, like the rest of the world; I don't understand you, I won't accept you as you are, I keep trying to make you into something you are not.

I promise to accept you if you will accept me. I am not sure I want to accept who you say you are, when I have reason to believe that this is a ruse to manipulate what happens between us. If you are really helpless about getting here on time, then we will have to change the terms between us. If you can't be relied on to get here on time, what new arrangements shall we make?

You don't answer. You pout. You just want it to be open; you will get here when you get here. Why am I being so petty about time? I don't feel that I am being petty. All we have are fifty precious minutes to spend together, and you seem to be uninterested whether we meet or don't meet, whether you get here ten, twenty or thirty minutes late. What are you saying about what you think of me and your therapy? Can you be telling me indirectly that it is not very important to you and that you don't think it is worthwhile? Why not tell me this directly so that we can talk about it?

Well, you grudgingly admit that you don't think it is going well and that you are not getting much out of it.

I ask how this is so, what do you want that is not happening, and you go on to say that you don't feel accepted, that even if I don't say something when you come late, you don't like the look on my face; that when you see that look you become sour and don't want to talk to me.

I wonder if you are setting me up by first coming late, then not recognizing that you may be trying to provoke me; if you may not be feeling guilty about being late and then trying to blame me by interpreting a look on my face without questioning me about it.

You really don't care to go on with the discussion. You came late today; your time is almost up and we haven't talked about anything important. You really had lots of things you wanted to tell me, and now there is no time.

I point out that you are blaming me again, that you take no

responsibility for getting here on time and no responsibility for what happens in the situation. If you had something you wanted to talk about, you could have interrupted at any time, but you decided to keep quiet until the end of the hour and then blame me for keeping you from talking about what you believed to be vital.

You don't answer. You are still angry and continue pouting. I remind you that I asked you three times for suggestions about what to do, what new arrangements you want to make about your lateness, and you have not bothered to answer. I ask you to think about this and let me know what you propose when we meet again.

I confess that I find all of this irritating, that I don't like to be a timekeeper, that I don't want to watch the clock. Yet when you repeatedly come late or not at all, you invite me to talk about it, and then you ignore what you have invited. I offer you an interpretation that what you are saying through the way you behave about time is what you feel toward me and your therapy: that I, it, we are not important enough to bother about or that we are too threatening to deal with by taking us seriously. So we stop for the day. I will be interested to see you next time so that we can go on with this and whatever else is important to you. Now I have to decide for myself what I want to do if you continue to be late, and I have my own private dialogue when you leave. I must make a judgment as to whether you want to continue therapy or if you are using this as a means of starting to leave. I must decide if I want to prevent you from leaving by letting the argument lapse. If I do so, what are the chances that it will immediately recur in another guise? If I think this will happen, what is gained by avoiding facing the issue now? If I decide to wait, there is a possibility that you will have become more committed to your therapy so that we can continue. On the other hand, I may simply be postponing the inevitable. Perhaps you are not ready for therapy at this point. You can run your life well enough and are not in a desperate condition. You are not terribly unhappy, just chronically dissatisfied, slightly sour. Maybe you need more time to continue in this way to see if it is worth it to you to make the effort to see me for regular sessions. Perhaps if we stop now you will recognize that you are not being forced to do anything, that you can decide to have therapy or not have therapy, to get to therapy or not get to therapy. You are in charge of your life and you can live it as you please.

I feel clearer myself and less annoyed. I believe it might be useful for you to stop therapy now so that you can decide if you really want it or not. I plan on telling you all this at our next session and leaving the decision up to you.

You decide that you really don't want to keep coming, that you don't want to deal with the issues in your life right now, that although you are unhappy, you can manage, and that perhaps later you will want to start again. I agree and indicate that when you do I will be willing to talk with you. I also offer the possibility that if you would rather see someone else at that time, though I would like to go on with you, I will be willing to give you the names of two other therapists.

You seem relieved, and I hope you can stop now without guilt. We part on a friendly basis. I have some regrets. My own private fantasy is that whoever needs therapy should have it. Yet I have to recognize that not everyone wants it or is ready to work at it. Still, my other fantasy is that if someone needs therapy I ought to be able to find a way to see that they can get it. Reluctantly I must admit my own limits. I can't reach everyone, particularly if they don't want to be reached. I could try harder if I wanted to here, but what would it cost me to blind myself to your message of wanting to stop so that I could protect my own fantasies that anyone who comes to me for therapy will want to continue, that anyone who needs therapy should have it, that I should be able to find a way to make therapy available to everyone who needs it? I recognize that I am indulging myself in my own fantasies and not recognizing my limitations, and so I stop, reasonably content to let you go.

Most people never get to a therapist's office at all. They *can cope* all right, and why bother with the rest of it? Oh, they may feel in the long hours of the night that something needs attending to, but, comes the dawn, all doubts are put aside.

Am I suggesting, then, that everyone needs therapy? No, not at all. Indeed, most people *can cope* and do so more or less successfully. The best reason for going to a therapist is because an individual wants to change. To do more than just cope, he wants to know himself better, to grow and develop, to find out who he is and how to live with that.

Most people are unwilling to undertake the self-confrontation involved in therapy. Either they are too frightened of what they will find, or what the therapist will help them to discover, or else they prefer to defend themselves against self-knowledge and not face the implications of such knowledge. My point is that I see only a select group—people who are willing to seek out a private therapist and undertake a course of self-knowledge and self-awareness with me.

What I am particularly interested in discussing here is what happens to even this select group. How serious are they and what happens as therapy progresses?

First of all, let me mention a special group, the quickies. I get a small number of people who start and quickly stop therapy in less than half a dozen sessions. Here are some examples of these in-and-outers:

Ralph was a middle-aged high-school teacher who had been in psychoanalysis for many years. He felt he finally had a grip on himself, although many of his original difficulties in life remained. He was lonely, unmarried, unhappy as a teacher, unhappy with his mother and her domination of his life. His new young girlfriend, whom he wanted to impress, suggested he try Gestalt Therapy. She told him she had gained a great deal from the experience. Ralph, eager to please and vaguely discontented with his lot, came to visit the miracle worker. We quickly established that Ralph was angry because despite all the time, money and effort he had spent in psychoanalysis, he had not turned into Prince Charming and his life was still incomplete in terms of satisfactions. At the same time, Ralph was clear that he was not eager to begin what he considered the long, exhausting, weary process of therapy again. He conceded that was not what he experienced with me, but he was not willing to see how valid a new approach might be.

I shared with him my thought that he made me think of a strong castle surrounded by a moat and that he felt secure but lonely behind his walls. He smiled and admitted that he ran his life this way but went on to say that he had no intention of giving up his moat or walls. I asked him to consider what was possible when he limited his contacts so thoroughly. But Ralph broke up with his new girlfriend after his next date, and this made it unnecessary to continue with his efforts to gain a new life for himself. He also discontinued his therapy. Clearly, then, Ralph came to therapy either to please his girlfriend or to look for a miracle. His own interest in therapy was long ago exhausted by his Freudian analysis of seven years, and he was prepared to accept the misery of his current life.

Steven was somewhat similar with regard to his condition in life: middle-aged, lonely, unmarried, unsuccessful as a lawyer. A friend convinced him to try Gestalt Therapy, and he made an appointment. Once several years ago he had visited a therapist on a few occasions, but he admitted that he didn't trust him, and he quickly dropped out of therapy. I asked him why he would trust me and he answered honestly that he did not. Indeed, he wanted to know if he was being recorded, what kind of notes I was keeping on him, who would see these nonexistent notes, etc. I asked him to inspect the premises for recording equipment, but he refused, saying that he believed he was being recorded anyway.

Our few sessions were painful. Steven insisted on telling me his "life story," but when I questioned him about any of it he refused to answer. When I suggested that what he wanted me to do was to sit and listen to whatever he told me, he objected, but when I asked questions he ignored me. Steven's story was simple enough: All his difficulties stemmed from problems at home with his father, his older brother, who was preferred, and his mother. Any difficulties he experienced could be traced to their treatment of Steven. Wearily and with misgivings I consented to listen to Steven's story. If I accepted that this was what he wanted to do, then perhaps I might gain some acceptance by going along with it. I should add that I did not deceive Steven about my own feelings. I told him that I wanted to get to know him and not his "story," but if he insisted on telling his story, then I would listen.

By the time he had finished his story he confessed that he had left out whole portions of the truth and had told me only one or two true occurrences, such as his embezzlements and disbarment. He then broke his next two appointments and finally called me up to inform me that he could no longer afford to pay for therapy because he was experiencing difficulties with his investments. I invited him to come in and talk, but I never saw him again.

My own guess is that Steven was so afraid of looking at himself and finding out what part he played in his own misfortunes that he could not tolerate the therapeutic situation. Rarely have I felt that a person talked *at* me rather than *to* me, rarely have I felt so much unwillingness to proceed in a session except at his own command. And then despite all this control, Steven felt too threatened and departed.

There are many variations on this theme of fear of what the therapy or the therapist will impose, and so a quick departure from therapy.

Henry was a social worker who had difficulty passing his exams, later in getting a job. He had been married once, divorced, and was now pretending to his parents that he was re-married but wanting to break up with his "second wife." Henry had been in several different types of therapy: rational therapy,

Horney analysis, several encounter groups. He stayed in therapy with me longer than any of the others (hurrah), but over and over I heard that nothing that happened penetrated beyond his intellectual understanding or else he rejected it because it was "ridiculous."

As therapy proceeded, I learned that Henry was extremely anxious and frightened, although on the surface, at a hefty 6'4", he tended to frighten others. He cursed frequently, drank freely, smoked three packs a day. As therapy proceeded, Henry became less anxious and frightened, but he maintained that this might have happened independently and therefore probably had nothing to do with his therapy. I suggested that he might also be frightened of me, but this was "ridiculous," and the most he could accept was that perhaps I had a point, but it was too intellectual for him to connect with. He had several dreams in which I threatened him or in which he was abusive toward me, but these too were only dreams and he could not connect with what was happening in the dream. I tried to reach Henry in every way I knew, and when I suggested to him that perhaps he was playing a game wherein I tried to reach him and he watched with pleasure as he refused to be reached, he laughed loudly and said that no such thing was possible.

I finally invited Henry to terminate since I shared with him the conclusion that he would not permit himself to take advantage of his therapy, and I could not in good conscience continue to pretend that he was in treatment. He did not fight me on this as he had on other interpretations, and so we parted. Later he wrote a letter and thanked me for my efforts on his behalf, and still later he spoke with a woman who he knew was in therapy with me and sent a message that someday he wanted to come back to therapy. At that time, I will gladly begin again.

Sophia was a senior at a prestigious women's college, having difficulty in studying at the beginning of the term. She insisted on seeing me immediately, and because my schedule was crowded she came at 7:00 A.M. She announced that she was having a "nervous breakdown" and proceeded in highly intelligent, lucid terms to discuss the nature of this breakdown.

I asked her what would be good about having a nervous breakdown, and she quickly informed me that she could withdraw from school, that her boyfriend would feel sorry for her and remove the emotional pressure he had been putting on her to be close, to be more loving, to give more to him. Her mother had had nervous breakdowns, and now it was her turn to get what she wanted this way. She did not want to have to go through her senior year and find out whether she had the potential that others kept telling her she possessed but which she doubted.

I suggested that if she wanted to withdraw from college this was possible, but it was not necessary to have a nervous breakdown to do so. Sophia was angry at this. She told me that what she wanted from me was what therapists were supposed to do: listen and then tell her what to do. We talked about other things too, but Sophia didn't come back, and I didn't expect her.

I learned subsequently that she did not have a nervous breakdown but she did withdraw from college. I am not sure what she will do about therapy.

Henry, Ralph, Sophia, Steven—what could I have done to continue to engage them in therapy? Probably nothing. Now that may sound heartless and self-protective perhaps, but it is not: I believe that none of these individuals was committed to the idea of therapy, that either they wanted something therapy could not provide honestly or they were unwilling to make the effort in their own behalf. Much as I might want to delude myself that each person who comes to see me must have therapy or must have me as his therapist, I have to be humbler. In order to function, I have to work with someone who is willing to meet me someplace where we can both be comfortable. The most serious person was Henry, but Henry could not part with basic distrust and his need to pull away from people. During the period in which we worked together, Henry was able to face his own passivity and accept it and later to cope with it, to recognize how he pushed people away, including his "second wife," and his parents, whom he had deceived, as well as me, and to be much more successful in his work. But he still felt anxious and unhappy, and although we parted I regret that I could not be there for him. I sent him to another therapist, and that relationship lasted less than two months. For Henry, being close was tantamount to being overwhelmed, and so minimal therapy was all he could tolerate.

The temptation of every therapist is to feel so good about himself that he comes to believe that he can treat every person who comes to his office, no matter what the situation. Technically, we might speak about omnipotence or narcissism, more humanly and in characterological terms we might speak of arrogance or *chutzpah,* but regardless of the term the situation remains: It is impossible to treat anyone without his cooperation. Thus, with regard to Sophia, Ralph, Henry or Steven, I humbly believe it made little difference what I did or did not do, that these individuals were not available to therapy. Now, if you belong to the school of the friends of psychotherapy and share the belief that anyone who enters an office is ready for therapy, you must count me a failure. But if you are more honest and less dogmatic, you will realize that it is not enough to enter a therapist's office to be in treatment. So sadly, reluctantly, unfortunately, I must conclude that I was helpless to aid these four people. Perhaps if I had been willing to pay each person to come to see me, if I had been willing to go to ask them to undergo treatment, we might have worked something out in some fashion. But then I would not have been faithful to my own belief of how I want to practice. I am free to set my terms of what makes sense to me, and they are free to accept or not accept those terms. If they can find better or more agreeable terms elsewhere, then so be it. If they want to return again at another time, then so be it. The initiative is theirs. My office door is open, my telephone is free.

Now, I have deliberately selected these four individuals to begin with because the issues are fairly clear-cut. In the following examples the issues are much more complex.

Alma's husband is a very successful corporate lawyer. He specializes in tax cases involving huge sums of money where his knowledge of the intricacies of the federal tax laws can change the profit picture of the large corporations he represents. He feels this work is incredibly demanding and originally came to me because of his high blood pressure and several "heart attacks" for which his cardiologist could find no physiological explanation.

Alma and George have been married for thirty years, have four children and six grandchildren. They seem to live the proper lives of Connecticut exurbanites: They drink too much, smoke too much, spend too much and party each weekend either at the country club or one another's houses. Alma's father was an enormously successful tycoon who made and lost fortunes, beat his wife when drunk and kept as many as three mistresses at a time. George, on the other hand, is extremely inhibited, except when he has had a few too many drinks. His older sister has spent her life in and out of mental hospitals; an older brother is an elegant homosexual who keeps a series of young, handsome and impoverished Algerians in Paris. George is ashamed of his flamboyant brother and his disturbed sister. George's mother lives alone and aloof in a Park Avenue apartment, protected by her maid and her doorman. He feels guilty about his mother and avoids her as much as possible.

Alma has more psychosomatic ailments than George, and they are even more mysterious: a dermatitis that appears and disappears with no apparent cause, menstrual periods lasting three weeks, a false pregnancy and migraine headaches since the age of seven.

Alma has already consulted six different therapists with no improvement: two Freudians (an orthodox male and a neo-Freudian female), a Jungian, a Sullivanian and most recently, in quick succession, a Reichian and a bioenergeticist. She has also been an adept of Gurdjieff, dianetics, transcendental meditation and biofeedback. When Alma is unhappy she likes to take a trip to Paris and buy a Renaissance bronze and St. Laurent dresses.

George has not previously been in therapy. His original skepticism was reinforced by the example of Alma's endless quest with little or no apparent change. However, his secretary had been seeing me for almost three years, and during that time her life was visibly altered. She first sought therapy because she was depressed by the death of her father. During treatment, once she had completed her mourning, she became more outgoing, began to date, got engaged, was able to experience orgasms for the first time, and after she married she quit her work to go back to graduate school to train in social work. She was an enthusiastic missionary for Gestalt Therapy, continued as a member of one of my groups after she stopped individual therapy and, during the three years I saw her, referred about a half dozen of her friends and acquaintances to me. George was impressed by all of the apparent movement in his former secretary's life, as well as by her constant paeans to Gestalt Therapy. When his cardiologist suggested he ought to consider psychotherapy for his "heart attacks" he chose not to consult Alma, who considered herself an expert, but his secretary. And so he came to me.

I liked George as a person. Despite his difficult family background and his unhappy marriage, he had continued in his career. Beneath his austere WASP exterior there was something boyish, but to see it I had to look quickly at his eyes or the corners of his mouth when he smiled. If he was aware that I was enjoying the unguarded look on his face it immediately disappeared.

Treatment was very difficult. He had accepted wholesale the Protestant Ethic as well as the manly code exemplified by Gary Cooper and John Wayne in their early movies. Feelings were taboo, feminine, nonexistent in adult males. What was *he* feeling? Nothing! What was nothing like? Don't be a damn fool! What was he feeling now, toward me? Anger? No, not anything!

I owned that it looked suspiciously like outrage, contempt, superiority. Well, perhaps, but what did that mean, what difference did it make? Was that what I meant by feelings? During sessions George drifted off, found that he had not heard what I had just said, could not remember what I said, even when I repeated it, could not remember from one session to the next what we had talked about, could not remember his dreams. Yet he paid his bill promptly on the last day of each month.

From George's point of view, he wanted to understand his "heart condition"; he wanted to puzzle through intellectually what was troubling him, and he assumed that that would be sufficient. Nonetheless, something somewhere was happening to him as a result of his group and private sessions. He started to become more interested in Alma sexually, while at the same time he began to quarrel with her in a more open way. Previously when they had disagreements he had sulked and contained his rage. Now he began to curse the way he had in the Army but had never dared to in civilian life. He also began to make love to her about once a week instead of about once a month.

Alma had been indifferent to George's therapy, since he had not consulted her in the choice of a therapist, but with these changes in George she became more curious. She questioned him about his sessions and about me. Finally she asked to begin therapy with me.

I work with couples as well as individuals, and I agreed to a consultation. Alma wore a lovely chiffon St. Laurent dress with pleats and a trailing scarf. I was very impressed with her chic. She spoke knowledgeably about her previous therapies but remained distant from me. She was intelligent but not as intelligent as she would have me believe; she faked or finessed a great deal. Our sessions quickly came to follow a pattern. Alma would bring me a dream that she felt she could interpret. I would accept her interpretation. Then as we continued I would try to lead her to explore the dream. Other facets of the dream would emerge.

Alma would be at once both excited and distressed—excited to come to some new awareness, distressed that she was not in charge, that she had revealed something she had not intended.

Alma claimed to become very fond of me, spent a good deal of her session praising me. I politely tried to demur, told her I was flattered, held back and was fairly bored by her using me as a means of keeping the therapy from progressing. She offered me concert tickets, brought in books, told me of smart new restaurants to visit. I told Alma I felt she was trying to woo and win me as an ally, perhaps against George, but she smiled and protested her innocence.

Meanwhile, she complained bitterly about George and made me aware of aspects of his personality I had not particularly noticed. I still aimed at neutrality between them, but gradually I learned that a real war was going on. George also complained about Alma, and so I asked each to pretend I was not seeing the other. I asked that each spend his session only in talking about himself and not about the other. I have worked with couples, as I indicated earlier, but this was a special situation where I found myself cast in the role of arbiter, judge, marriage counselor, referee.

I tried to point out the war, but either I was naïve, the only one who was not aware of it, or else they were not interested. What each wanted was a friend and ally to change the balance of power, to assure victory. I tried to point out what the war was doing to each, what the terms were, how self-defeating these kinds of battles were, but I got nowhere. So I switched tactics and spoke of the strength of hatred, of the excitement, once passion has cooled, in defeating the other, how inflicting pain is often an acceptable switch from giving pleasure. Still I got nowhere. I came to realize that I too was as much enemy as ally, that together Alma and George would discuss me and support their own resistances. Alma and George had spent thirty years fighting each other and were not about to give up their warfare. Each had insulated himself from close friendships or meaningful affairs in order to give himself over to the struggle against the other. And each week there was a new cause for argument. George wanted to go to Aspen for Easter vacation; Alma wanted to go to the Aegean. Alma wanted to buy a small Braque; George said they couldn't afford it. George felt he had to attend the funeral of a great-aunt in Philadelphia; Alma was too incapacitated by her menstrual flow. Alma wanted to launch a visiting tachiste painter, but George said he was too tired, didn't like or understand tachism and didn't want any large parties.

I spoke of compromise, taking turns. I was ignored. I spoke of underlying anger, of using anything at hand to promote a fight. I was ignored. I asked for a moratorium on each other. I was ignored. Gradually Alma realized that I refused to take her part, and on occasion, just once or twice, she laid into me in the same way George reported she did to him. I accepted her anger and asked her to tell me what else she was angry with me about, but she pulled back. How could she be angry with anyone who was so sweet and understood her so well? Shortly thereafter she stopped coming without even arranging to discuss her decision to leave therapy. I had joined the long list of her previous therapists. In my case, however, I was the only one who also saw George.

George was relieved when Alma stopped coming. He had never liked the idea of my getting to know her and regretted that he had consented to her coming too. However, his use of therapy remained minimal. He never forgot appointments, always came on time, always paid some slight attention, and then could retain nothing of what had transpired. By the time he was ready to leave each session, he could not remember what we had talked about.

I found means to convince George that indeed he could remember what we had talked about, that he could even remember formulations we had come to. He continued to insist that his chest pains were really not psychogenic, and occasionally he would return to his cardiologist for still another test. Despite all this his chest pains decreased in severity and the "attacks" came less frequently. Yet our sessions remained as grim as ever. Finally, Alma convinced George to consult a psychiatrist who would give him both tranquilizers and digitalis to use whenever he felt his chest pains. George felt very guilty when he came to talk about it, but there was no doubt that he preferred to take medicine. We agreed to stop treatment, though George was so guilty that he even suggested that he see both of us.

Two years later I ran into Alma at the Museum of Modern Art. She kissed me on both cheeks, and then she told me that she had just begun therapy once more, with an orthodox Freudian who was very eminent and very expensive, and that George and she were still together; he was still with his psychiatrist and he was taking more pills as well as a course of vitamins and supervised athletics.

Then there was Clark. I saw Clark for three months, but it was almost as if I never saw him at all. We never connected in any significant way. Clark had had a series of men in his life, and they had all either died or left him. First his father died when he was six. His mother remarried, but his stepfather left when the marriage failed. In high school Clark became friendly with the local minister, but when Clark's faith in Christianity left him, his relationship with the minister ended. Clark could not concentrate sufficiently to do college work, and he got a series of part-time jobs that lasted for only a matter of weeks before he was fired or stopped going. Then during the Sixties he became a follower of one of the early charismatic figures of the civil-rights protest movement. He became totally involved, completely subordinating himself to the needs of the leader and the movement. He went to the South to organize sit-ins, work on freedom marches and even smuggle guns and ammunition when violence began. Somehow (I could never get the story straight) he had

had a falling-out with the civil-rights leader, and he abandoned the civil-rights movement shortly after his gunrunning adventures.

Then he returned to religion, but this time it was of the Eastern variety. He became a follower of a sect that believed that the leader was God reborn. When I met Clark he chanted, prayed, attended meetings twice a week and sought enlightenment. Why, then, did he come to see me? He had seen a number of therapists since he was a boy. I was the fourth. A friend of his in the East Village had suggested he come to see me. His mother in New Mexico would pay the bills, he assured me.

Clark felt he might as well come for therapy because he didn't know what else to do. He found his religion vital and important, but aside from attending meetings and praying each day, he hardly left his house. He had a girlfriend of sorts; he had never made love to her, and she had just come from a stay in a mental hospital and was not sure that she was not going back. She went to prayer meetings with him and sometimes they had coffee afterward.

Our sessions were painful. Often he wouldn't talk, his eyes would glaze over, his face twitch and his hands tremble. When I asked him what was happening, what he was feeling, he said he was lost in his dreams, and when I asked him to tell them to me, he said he had forgotten them or that he couldn't trust me.

I would question Clark and he would answer my questions. If I tried to find out how he was feeling, he would try to avoid answering by quoting his religious leader. When I would quote his leader back to him, he would smile faintly. He was supposed to quote to me, not I to him. The purpose of the leader was to permit him to be with me and yet not be with me. It was not fair for me to take his leader seriously and try to enter into the system he was telling me about. I tried to talk to Clark about all of the men who had meant something to him and then disappeared. He said he knew about all that but that he couldn't trust anyone that way any longer. I told him that I understood how he felt that he couldn't trust me but that maybe in time things would be different. He gave no answer.

When we talked about his father he almost cried, but he stopped himself and then withdrew. We talked about the idea of a job and how he felt about working. During the day he usually stayed at home, sometimes writing in his diary, occasionally watching television. He was afraid to go out much because he thought the FBI might still be after him because of his gunrunning activities, and he was somewhat fearful that by watching television he would be brainwashed into the American way of life. He didn't take drugs because he said he knew he couldn't handle them, that they would make him too crazy and, as he put it, too paranoid.

Clark began to take trips to Maine and miss sessions. Sometimes he let me know; other times he did not. Did he miss the sessions, was he trying to get me angry by not phoning, was he trying to worry me, to see if I cared? These were my ideas, so I would have to answer them for myself. Could we go on this way together if he took no responsibility for what he did? Did I want him to stop coming, because if so, then he would oblige. What did he want to do? He didn't know. What difference did it make? He couldn't say.

The worst of the winter was over, and in Maine someone he knew told him of a hunter's shack that was available for ten dollars a month rent out of hunting season. There was a wood stove, a small community of the same religious leader only fifteen miles away and a good highway nearby from which he could hitchhike back and forth. Although the weather was still cold, he had decided to go and live there. It was cheap, the FBI was probably not active there, and in the religious community he might find friends. The vibes in the city were too poisonous. And so he left.

I asked him to write, but I never heard from him. He almost

cried at the last session, but his tears had no meaning for him. I felt he was paying me back for all the other men who had left him, and now he was leaving me first. Perhaps that was as much as I could do for him, to let him have the experience of leaving someone rather than of being left. I am not sure.

I think I had more difficulty with Tom than anyone else I ever saw. He was loud, brash, aggressive, manipulative—a business-man. Underneath this façade of boasting, pushing, he felt weak, helpless, hopeless. I could understand all of this, but somehow it made no difference to me. I could not find any sympathy in myself for his condition. When he was obnoxious I could not extend myself beyond what was so obviously in front of me, to contact what else was there but not so readily apparent. If I were content to give him only my anger, he would have been happy to leave therapy. He distrusted anything but a profit and loss state-ment anyway.

But why was I so ready to take sides against him? What prevented me from contacting his fragile, vulnerable, isolated life? I decided to seek a consultation with another therapist for my own sake, to learn what about Tom upset me so much. I discovered that regardless of the merit of my anger with Tom, I found its source elsewhere. When I myself played Tom I found that instead of the figure of Tom I was so angry with, I found the figure of my mother. And not even my mother. Instead, I found myself dealing with my angriest feelings with the most negative picture of my mother I had available. It was my mother in her worst moments and I at my very angriest that Tom had provoked in me. It was no wonder that I had so little sympathy for him. I still didn't like what he was putting forth, but I no longer had to punish either of us because he reminded me so much of myself at my most helpless with my mother at her worst. Here I had almost failed because of my own unfinished situations from the past, and once I came to realize this I was in a position to take precaution. We went forward from that point, and I could then let myself feel greater sympathy and empathy for Tom in his own trap.

Kate I lost to God. We had worked together for a little more than a year. She had a miserable life. Her father had seduced her when she was twelve years old, and after having an affair with her for the next year and a half he had run away with another woman. Kate was so upset that she went off to a mental hospital for the next nine months. During her hospitalization her mother learned what had happened between her husband and Kate and never forgave Kate for it. Kate dropped out of high school after about another year of schooling and then began to float through Greenwich Village. She began to specialize in older poets and had a succession of brief affairs. Gradually she started to write poetry herself. Usually she didn't work but moved in with her protector and desultorily kept house. She began to drink. She floated in and out of therapy for three to six months at a time, usually availing herself of the variety of outpatient clinics that New York provides.

By the time she came to see me she was thirty-three. She was living with a poet once more, and he seemed to be genuinely fond of her. She had been with him for two years, and he had said that he would pay for her therapy. She had decided to come to see me because a friend of hers had been in treatment with me and suggested that her ability to stick with her painting had improved. Kate wanted to be able to write.

She looked much older than her thirty-three years; her drinking showed. She felt very guilty about the three abortions she had undergone during the last ten years and was still in conflict over what had happened with her father more than twenty years before.

Kate had a lot of warmth and vitality and I enjoyed working with her. I found her tough, unsentimental view of life appealing. She would collapse suddenly. She would feel helpless and demanding. She was sure that she was doomed and that nothing could work out for her. She distrusted her ability as a poet, her ability to love, to be a mother. She felt doomed.

Yet she continued to come to see me, and we talked about her guilt and shame over what had happened so long ago. We talked about her wanting a family of her own, and she even confessed that she wanted to marry the man she was living with. For the first time in over ten years she was able to visit her mother to see if there was any possible basis for a friendship between them. Kate was not too sure, but she was impressed by her mother's offer of a loan to get some new clothes and a new hairdo. Kate was also surprised to find herself so loving toward her younger stepbrother, whom she had never seen before.

Kate also began to get some free-lance, part-time writing assignments. She had never earned any money by her writing, and at first she was frightened and thrilled. She began to feel that she might earn a living or at least pay her own way. Occasionally she would still get drunk, pick up an older man and sleep with him. And then the roof caved in.

Kate's poet got sick and went to a hospital. She felt that it must be her fault, that God was punishing her for her wickedness and both she and her man would have to suffer. On her own while he was in the hospital, lonely and frightened, she drank to escape. Once drunk, she sought an older man to comfort her in bed, with the same repetition of guilt the next day. Meanwhile, her lover had been diagnosed as having cancer. The recommendation was radiation therapy. Kate started talking to God and his angels. Sometimes they were real men whom she met as she wandered about the city, and after she talked to them for a while she realized that they only pretended to be mortals but were really angels in disguise. At other times they appeared to her in a blaze of light, and there was no doubt as to who they were.

Kate talked to me about her experiences with God and the angels. She felt that I would disbelieve her, and I answered that although I was somewhat skeptical, I would try to be open to her own experiences. We talked about her loneliness with her lover in the hospital and her fear about the coming radiation therapy. We talked about her feelings of guilt over sleeping with other men and the feelings that she had brought on this punishment to both her and her lover. She said that she would have to talk to her celestial friends and see what they thought. Her appearance at sessions became erratic, and then she finally came in one day and said that God had told her that she could not come to see me any more, that I could not be trusted.

I asked her to continue to come and see me, that I was sure that if she really wanted to, then her God would not object, but she shook her head. She cried, asked to be forgiven, promised to give up liquor, and then she left. I kept in touch with her lover, who subsequently recovered from his cancer with the aid of the radiation treatments. Kate is still with him, but she has stopped writing and stopped drinking. When friends ask her about therapy she says that it is too difficult for her to manage, that she doesn't have the strength for it. She no longer talks to God and his angels, nor does she talk about marriage. She wants to sit tight and not rock the boat. She quotes me as saying that to be in therapy means to be willing to take risks, and she is not.

Part Two

GROUP THERAPY

6 . The Group Meets

What happens in a group? Everything. Anything. Not quite. No one has ever fucked in a group that I have run, although I was not always sure that they might not. People have had physical fights, although there were no broken bones. And some people have fallen asleep. Usually, though, we "work." I'll explain what that means a little later.

At the beginning of the group, people do what anyone does at the start of any meeting. They chat idly, someone eats an apple, another smokes, some gossip. There is occasional laughter, some of it nervous.

I try to greet each person as he enters, to gain contact, to see where each person is. Usually, I am preparing coffee, tea or fruit juice, setting up glasses, cups, and, in my busy work, I avoid extended contact. Occasionally someone slips over and says, I want to work tonight. Again, that word *work*. During this period before the group starts, as members arrive and sit down, they also begin to prepare themselves. *Prepare* is a strange word perhaps. What I mean is that just as an audience prepares for the beginning of a play by awaiting the opening of the curtain, just as the auditorium becomes hushed and all eyes become accustomed to the lights dimming and the stage becomes the focus of attention, so members of the group prepare for their own dramas that are about to unfold. And just as an actor prepares for going onstage by sinking into his part, so group members prepare for dropping the polite, social masks that govern so much of their behavior in everyday life and prepare to confront themselves and others in a more honest and direct manner. This is one aspect of "work," and in this way everyone in the group works.

In individual sessions I find a similar kind of preparation. My office is on a fifth-floor walkup in a brownstone, and many people find the walk up the stairs a useful opportunity to prepare for entry into their session. Often they find themselves filled with thoughts and feelings they had not been aware of before their climb, and they arrive at my door fresh with all kinds of grist for their mill. Similarly, sometimes at the beginning of a session, a person may prepare by settling down, by getting comfortable, starting a cigarette, sitting quietly, searching into himself (herself) and then beginning. Group members who arrive late often report that they miss this opportunity to orient themselves to the session—that they literally burst into what is going on without having had a chance to prepare themselves to focus on what is happening within themselves.

They then may find themselves slightly disoriented as the group proceeds, just as if they had turned on the television set in the middle of a program, only the program that is featured is "This Is Your Life." Sometimes the latecomers sit silently, trying to catch up, flashing backward, trying to fill in gaps; sometimes they excuse themselves and ask for the information they lack; sometimes they jump right in and take their chances.

Lateness is a problem for me. When I was a professor I began class five minutes after the hour, and that was that. Each student had the responsibility for getting himself to class on time, and I had the option to close the door to latecomers, to be sarcastic about their tardiness, to ignore them. Now I am faced with the need to be "therapeutic." For the most part people are on time for individual sessions. But a group is different. We can begin at any time, as long as there are just two of us. Unless someone is chronically late, I prefer to spend time in the group on other matters than housekeeping and bookkeeping, like timekeeping, but if someone feels keenly about tardiness, then we go ahead and work on this.

I have finished puttering with coffee, and now the group members have arranged themselves. The most frightened, the most isolated, find armchairs to sit in, safe from close physical contact with others. The more relaxed members, the members who like to be touched, pick someone to sit next to and hold hands, stroke one another, sprawl with, massage. This contact between members is largely free of gender. In the group, men feel free to sit next to men and hold hands and embrace; women are free to hug, snuggle together on a large club chair, stroke hair. If there is a couple in the group, a husband may sit on one sofa, holding hands with one of the women in the group, and the wife may sit on another sofa, close to whomever she chooses.

The atmosphere of the group is free in other ways. I don't expect that each and every group member can be attentive during the length of the session to all that is happening. At times someone grows bored, even falls asleep, leafs through a magazine, talks to his neighbor. Each person is free to do as he pleases, but then each group member is also responsible for what he does, so that at any moment someone who objects to someone who falls asleep or talks can call him on it and the other must be prepared to deal with it in any way he pleases. Thus the group does not present the chance to say, "I can do anything I want to and it doesn't make any difference," but "I can do whatever I want to but others have a right to respond to what I am doing and let me know about it." I try to have as few rules as possible about what is expected behavior so that individuals are free, on the one hand, to experiment with what they are comfortable with and to widen the range of their experience and behavior and, on the other, to use what happens in the group as a means of broadening the therapeutic experience. Just as in the individual sessions, everything that happens may be grist for the therapeutic mill, though the range is wider in the group.

In this connection, some members may want to have sex with

me, and much as I may be flattered or repelled, I refrain from doing so. However, group members are free to make their own decisions with one another in this matter. I am not their policeman either in session or out, but I do ask them if they become sexually involved with another member of the group that they do not use what develops within their relationship as a means of withdrawing from therapy, once the going gets rough between them. Sometimes one group member will start to sleep with another and then use the failure of the relationship as an excuse to drop out of therapy. However, on the few occasions when this has happened, I could content myself with the awareness that the person dropping out had a history of dropping out of therapy. What these people are doing is creating a situation in which they can maintain a fantasy, and then when the fantasy doesn't work out the way they want, they withdraw from the entire situation. But then, again, from my point of view, this is similar to what had prompted them to withdraw from therapy in previous experiences.

On the other hand, I have had group members who explored their homosexual feelings with one another and who did not withdraw from therapy despite great difficulties as the relationship became unsatisfactory or as they were assailed by feelings of shame or guilt. Similarly, I have had members who began a love affair that did not last but that was useful to them for the greater knowledge they gained about their own responses and who stayed with the group throughout their liaison. As I indicated earlier, I could make rules about what members can and can't do, but then how could I enforce them? If members wanted to fuck without my permission, I suppose I could throw them out of the group if I found out. What good this would do them from a therapeutic point of view I am not sure; it would surely offer me an opportunity to be stern, authoritarian, and offer them an opportunity to be guilty. If I would be willing to take all this on and not throw them out of the group, then perhaps I would have a new therapeutic lever to work with. But I am not all that concerned in a moralistic way about what people do in bed with one another. I *am* willing to talk about what meaning sex has for anyone and what feelings are attached thereto. If someone is trying to provoke me by sleeping with a group member or to embarrass me by making a pass at me, then I feel free to talk about this without having to moralize or threaten exile. So, on occasion, group members will sleep together or even group members from different groups will sleep together, and this is just one of the things we can talk about if we think it is important, just as we can talk about who sits in a corner by himself or who never helps me clean up the coffee cups once a session is finished or who is avoiding working within the group.

I ordinarily wait a few minutes beyond the time at which we have agreed to meet, and then I indicate who will not be present and for what reasons. Matthew is in Hong Kong on a business trip, Erica's mother is sick and she flew home to be with her, Sidney has the flu, Henry has a deadline and will try to be here, although he may be a little late.

To me, a group meeting is as important as a private session. I expect each person to attend unless there is a very good reason. I take the meaning of therapy very seriously, and, even though in each session or meeting we may joke and laugh, I want everyone to be clear about the basic importance of our "work."

After pointing out who is absent and why, there is a silence. I either wait for someone to begin or I ask, Would anyone like to "work"? There is usually a good deal of tension and a lot of evading contact with my eyes.

I am notorious for trying to sniff out who would like help by an inspection of each face, by looking into someone's eyes, by attending to tone and rhythm. He who would avoid "work" avoids me. Most often someone volunteers or else agrees when I invite him/her. Sometimes no one volunteers, and then I invite someone and he refuses. No, not tonight. At this point the group may offer mild pressure. You haven't worked for some time now. Why not? There must be something. If the person is firm that he doesn't want the opportunity to work, then he is free not to. We try to make as few rules as possible.

The rules, which can of course be broken: To be as honest as possible in what you are feeling and thinking. To come regularly, on time. To be willing to "work," to be willing to risk, to try new things. To pay your bill. These are, to my knowledge, the rules, and from here we are on our own.

Harry would like to "work," but he doesn't know about what. As a warmup, as a means of his contacting his own feelings, as a means of clarifying where he is, I ask him to tell each of us one thing that he doesn't want to work on. He surprises himself with the ease with which he marches around the room and rapidly states, I don't want to work on my anger, I don't want to work on my relationship with my mother, I don't want to work on how I avoid work, I don't want to work on my feelings about sex, about my marriage, my loneliness, my need to get sick every time I face a crisis.

I ask innocently, although by now everyone knows the technique, Which is the item you don't want to work on the most? and after I have the reply I answer, All right, why don't we work on that? Yes, some of this can become ritualized, and, yes, the person can cheat and select something he doesn't want to work on. But then the rest of us are free to challenge him if we feel he is putting us off by a safe topic, and this too becomes grist for our mill.

Once Harry has arrived at a topic, we are then faced with how to proceed. In the previous example, where Harry agreed to work but was unable to articulate his choice, we dealt with his resistance by joining it, by inviting him to bring up the areas toward which he felt the greatest resistance and then to use this as a means of selection. With his choice of topic, we are next faced with how to proceed, how to contact Harry's feelings and thoughts.

As a means of facilitating this process, we invent *ad hoc* an "experiment." We prefer the term *experiment* rather than *exer-*

cise because an exercise is usually something done repetitively and mechanically to strengthen a particular skill or build an ability. An experiment is an honest attempt to find something out by trying a new technique, a means of learning by risking the security of established techniques for the freshness and insecurity of that which is new and untried. The thrill of the experiment is first to devise a method that will help Harry to take the next step, to gain a further sense of where he is so that he can become unstuck and proceed further. Harry decides he wants to work on how anxious he feels when he faces his students.

Harry begins by telling us of his feelings of inadequacy as a teacher, how he fears his students' reactions, despite the fact that his annual evaluations are glowing. I invite him to be one of his students and to offer a reaction he would like to have. Harry swells as one of his students and gives an exaggerated portrait of himself as the consummate teacher. He has shifted from feeling weak and helpless to being puffed up with pride and vanity. Someone points out the contrast between feeling small and large, weak and strong. Harry quickly associates to his feelings of sexual inadequacy both in terms of penis size and performance. Since we have dealt with these feelings in earlier group meetings, and since we know these feelings are still unfinished for Harry, we wait. Harry then associates to his dead father, with whom he still feels competitive. We ask Harry to pick someone to play his father, and without hesitation he selects Richard, an aggressive man with similar unresolved feelings toward his own father.

Richard quickly invents a script to reduce Harry. He interrogates Harry about his day at school when he was a graduate student. He flogs Harry verbally, and Harry cowers. Richard loses himself in his role as sadistic parent and becomes even more abusive. Harry continues to cringe. I interrupt, and Harry and Richard reverse roles and play the same scene. Richard is now deeply involved in his own difficulties with his father and begins to weep. I leave working with Harry and turn my attention to Richard, who regales us with lurid anecdotes of his father's brutality in the past. Richard alternately rages and cries. Some-one points out how much pleasure Richard is enjoying as he wallows in his own distress. He ignores this. In past sessions Richard has portrayed Cotton Mather inveighing against sin, John Wayne winning the West, a helpless child being nourished by the members of the group, a mourning son saying Kaddish and finally burying his father. These techniques have helped to some extent in aiding Richard to loosen his rigid sense of right and wrong, to accept his own needs, to feel independent of his father, to feel his own strength. Nonetheless, he continues to hold on to his struggle with his father and to treat much of his current experiences as a re-enactment of the past.

I invite Richard to take responsibility for his decision to live in the past, to tell us what he gets from hanging on to his involve-ment with his father to the exclusion of what is happening currently. He points out the pleasure of being a victim: someone else is to blame, not him; he is innocent, he is unjustly accused. He explains how he has an opportunity to vent his feelings of rage and know they are justified; he points to the safety of having a closed script available so that all new experience can be assimi-lated immediately in terms of the old; he is aware of the ease of isolating himself from what may be threatening now by replaying an old scene, etc., etc. He appears calmer and more reassured. Someone also suggests that even in his whole emotional display this evening he may have been trying to elicit sympathy and enjoying self-pity as a further means of withdrawing from contact with members of the group, of holding us at bay with a rich emotional and verbal production that will intimidate us. Richard laughs in an open way and confesses that he has enjoyed his performance but adds that much of it was real also. He did intend to use it to push us away, but he also felt some parts of it genuinely. He owns up to the fact that he is clear about how much he gets from maintaining his involvement with his father and avers he is still not ready to let it go.

Where is Richard's breakthrough? Well, he's already had half a dozen years of psychoanalysis, and I doubt that he is going to have one. I think it will be more useful for Richard to have a number of experiences with the group and me in which he can try out a lot of the knowledge he has but which is still too intellectual. He needs to make it a part of himself, and here in the group he can practice until he is comfortable with it.

Some therapists are always pushing for breakthroughs, striving for the sudden, dramatic rebirth. I am more skeptical and cautious. If new forms of integration spontaneously emerge, then I am pleased and delighted; but if they do not, then I am not disappointed. If I try to get a person not to become the victim of his high expectations, then I provide a poor example when I myself pressure him for a breakthrough. Should I push him in this way, then he quickly finds a passive means to thwart us both—by deliberately not moving.

I am also suspicious of breakthroughs for other reasons. I am against the concept of measurement that they imply. Too many people are self-consciously measuring their growth, counting the number of insights they received per session, charting their gains. I want no part in these attempts to quantify the value of therapy by reference to statistical tables of growth and rate of breakthroughs.

I also find that the notion of breakthrough brings with it the thought of "breaking." Too many people fear that what happens in therapy is that they are "shrunk" and that they will be "broken" down. From my point of view, the blocks are important parts of what a person has constructed as a means of living his life. I want to know how they are used and what value they have. I am not so eager to throw away so quickly what has been built so laboriously. Often the blocks represent frozen, rigidified sources of creativity and energy which when thawed become wonderful means of building new ways of living. I would rather not throw away the time-consuming, laborious exploration of the blocks and strive for some new, quick method of instant transfiguration.

I also object to the notion of breakthroughs because they relate to the concept of progress. Some therapists, I think, trap themselves by keeping a kind of personal box score on how well a person is progressing. If he makes gains, that is good. If he doesn't, that is bad. If he has made a gain and then slipped back, that is worse. Aside from the trap of measurement, which I referred to above, I question this whole way of thinking about what is happening to a person. If a person has made a gain, then it is because something within him has been freed so that he can try new methods or because his situation is altered so that he is free to explore new means. If he returns to older patterns that do not work as well, then very likely he is under some kind of threat, either within himself or from his situation, and has taken the means to deal with it that may not work too well but will afford him some measure of safety or comfort. To label this "regression" or "backsliding" or lack of progress is to miss the point or rather to get lost in the therapist's need (or the person's) to find success everywhere, to conquer through victory.

Sometimes a person achieves a new mode only to find that the cost is too high, that he prefers his old ways, that he needs more time to live through what he gets out of his old ways or that he gets too many gratifications in spiting himself or his therapist to go further at this time. Why not let a person be right now, yes, here and now, where he is without having to judge him with the label of progress or backsliding, and why not let him see how he feels, what he thinks, look at what he is getting out of it and what he feels is missing? And then if new, sudden forms of reorganization occur, fine; but if not, then that is fine too. I am willing to abandon a predetermined view of what therapy or a person's life ought to be. The Protestant Ethic will not forgive me, and I know I am un-American, but I am prepared to live with that.

I turn back to Harry. He has not felt neglected by our attending to Richard's needs. Indeed, he was deeply moved by Richard's working. He and Richard exchange some feelings from their role-playing episodes. One of the other men in the group asks Harry to consider how in other areas of his life he is trapped by the dilemma of needing to assert his own power when he feels weak.

At this point I ask Harry to stand up and walk around the room. He does so. I ask him to describe himself, how he walks, what he feels like. He recognizes that his shoulders are pulled back like a caricature of a soldier's; his arms dangle limply at his sides. I ask him to experiment with finding other ways of holding his upper torso. I mimic his stance so that he can see it more clearly, and I report how much tension I feel in my shoulder blades as I hold myself in the same way.

I then ask Harry to walk some more and to describe what happens in his lower torso and his legs. Is he aware of how he retracts his pelvis so that his genitals are pulled back? He forces each leg out in a kind of strut that begins in the buttocks so that he looks like a kind of rooster. At the same time he somehow shuffles so that his feet do not appear to touch the ground, as if he were doing a dance. Harry is an intellectual who has neglected his body. My guess is that he has now worked enough this evening in terms of becoming aware of how his difficulties in teaching are related to his need to get others to confirm his worth, something he withholds from himself. To go further at this point is to be out of touch with how much Harry can take in at one time. I suggest that he continue on his own to explore his usual method of walking and that he experiment with finding other kinds of walks that are more comfortable. I promise that we will work on his relations to his body another time in greater detail.

Douglas is a new member of the group. He has watched all of the emotionality of the encounter between Harry and Richard with curiosity and terror. I ask him to tell the members of the group what he would like from the group, why he has come. I am not so much interested in his answers so much as how he deals with my question. Doug first gives a vague answer, a standard answer. He wants to be with people, to learn to relate, to find out about himself. When I press him for details—how he relates now, what he wants to find out about himself—he becomes vague. I point out his evasion, and Doug becomes silent. I ask him if he feels criticized, and he admits that he does. I explain that in Gestalt Therapy we expect a person to be responsible for himself, that if Doug is being vague, he should take responsibility for that. If he is unaware he is vague, I ask him to see if he can contact his vagueness. Until he is aware of what he is doing and can take responsibility for it, it is unlikely that he will be able to change it in any way. Indeed, until he is aware of what he is doing and what he receives from his acts, he will have little ability to see whether he wants to change or stay the way he is. I then explain that my job is to help him become aware of what he is doing, that he has a choice of taking this as a form of criticism in which I blame him or accepting my observation as something he can work with, to check on whether it makes sense.

My small lecture is finished and I ask Doug how he feels now. He tells me that he feels a little better but that he is still tense. I ask Doug to tell me more about his tension, where he feels tense, how he feels tense. Doug says that he feels very tight in his chest, as though he were being squeezed. I ask him if he is aware of his breathing, to describe it. He looks at me with surprise—Isn't that a foolish question?—pauses and tells me that he is barely breathing. I tell him that one way of becoming tense is to stop breathing. I invite him to experiment with other ways of breathing. He tries short, quick breaths and says that he is becoming dizzy, lightheaded. I point out that he is close to hyperventilating and that this is another way of making himself anxious. Then Doug gulps huge amounts of air, as if he were swimming and about to dive under water. He still feels anxious. I direct him to expel all of the air from his abdomen so that none remains. He does so, and Doug learns that if he pushes all of the air out of his abdomen he will automatically take a deep breath. He begins to breath more naturally and I ask him how he feels. Better but still tense. He feels a tingling. I ask him to consider that he might be excited. He breaks into a quick, full smile. He is excited; he had not let himself know it. He relaxes and feels pleased with himself. I give another small lecture, that tension can sometimes be a form of blocked excitement, that sometimes people are frightened of or threatened by being excited and that in order to control their excitement they clamp down on it. The feelings of excitement then are clamped down, are then converted into anxiety.

I pause myself at this moment for a breath of air and note that the room is filled with cigarette smoke.

A debate begins—the smokers against the non-smokers. The non-smokers are a new, hearty breed who have become less passive during the last decades. They no longer want to put up with inhaling smoke from others' cigarettes. The smokers, somewhat defensive, plead for tolerance, even for indulgence. The smoke gets thicker and the butts mount. As the group becomes more relaxed, the door is opened—the hell with whatever someone passing through the corridor will hear; it is more important to get some fresh air for both smoker and non-smoker.

One group worked out a compromise. Each smoker voluntarily limits himself to one cigarette per half hour unless he is "working"; then he can become a chimney. Some therapists refuse to permit the person working to smoke at all, but I do not arbitrarily want to deprive someone of his props. On occasion, however, I may ask a smoker to forgo his usual cigarette. Here my decision is deliberately made to suit the situation and is not a closed rule.

I myself do not smoke—that is, I smoke about half a dozen cigarettes a week. The toilet is always available as a refuge. When I was in grade school I always raised my hand "to go," regardless of the state of my bladder, so that I could escape the classroom for about five to ten minutes. And now the same thing happens in the group. Members drift in and out of the toilet when they need a break. In some ways the toilet functions like the water cooler in an office; when people want an excuse to absent themselves from their desks and yet not arouse guilt, then the bladder becomes full or the bowels beckon.

What is sometimes funny is that as one person approaches the end of his "work," the person who will succeed him, either through having asked to reserve time or else when I have indicated that it would be appropriate for him to work, lo, this is the time that nature calls, and the group finds itself waiting for the member who is now closeted. So we all have a break, a pause while the next person prepares for his ordeal.

Now Louise is getting annoyed with me. She thinks that if I am a Gestalt therapist I should not give lectures, that I am too intellectual. This is an ongoing battle I have with Louise. Louise has moved from Big Sur to New York and has, from my point of view, confused some of Fritz Perls' later writings with all of Gestalt Therapy. Louise is against any interpretations at all, although I ask her to read *Gestalt Therapy Verbatim* carefully to see whether or not there are not lots of interpretations. She is against any kind of theorizing, any kind of teaching. I ask Louise if she has invented all of her own way of living, and, if she has not, where she learned it. Louise hates any kind of formality, any established ways of doing things; she wants to be free. She prefers to forget that she *learned* how to speak; she did not invent English. She *learned* how to cook; she even *learned* how to paint. I ask Louise to invent her own language right now and communicate with us. She quickly accepts the task, mumbles guttural sounds, begins to make gestures. Someone points out that she is using sign language, that she has *learned* this too. Louise becomes more agitated, and I ask her to invent her own sign language as well. She tries, and we are amused by some of her creations, but no one has any idea of what she is trying to say.

Then I ask Louise how she feels. She is alert and excited. She had thought she would feel free by escaping the tyranny of language; she felt thrilled by the possibility of creating her own, but then as she tried to work with it she felt oppressed by the difficulty of communicating from scratch. Then when she saw sign language taken away, she felt isolated and frustrated. Louise feels she has taken on more than she can handle.

I ask her what is so offensive about taking from others, whether it be language or traditions. Louise gets quickly angry: because then you have to be grateful, because you then are supposed to obey the rules, because you lose your freedom. I ask Louise who it was that she had to obey, who it was she felt she had to be grateful to. She spontaneously says, My mother. Louise bitterly recounts how she feels her mother restricted her as a child, how her mother wanted her to be demure, sweet, how her mother dressed her in pinafores, later in sweater sets, how her mother tried to get her to accept the affluent values of suburban California. I suggest to Louise that her mother may have had this ability to influence her in the past, when Louise was small or felt tied by a sense of obligation, but now she is an adult and can make her own decisions. Louise retorts quickly, You're damned right. I'll live just the way I want. I ask Louise, Just how is that? Tell each of us how you choose to live now.

Louise informs us that she doesn't want to eat at a set time, dress in a set way, live by set rules. I point out that she is not telling us what she wants but what she doesn't want. She pauses in anger, then reflects and goes on. She says defiantly, I want to sleep late, to fuck, to get drunk, to drive fast, to be sloppy. I ask her who would be most upset and she shouts, My mother, that bitch. I point out that Louise seems to want those things most which have been forbidden or which her mother disapproves of most.

Helena asks, If that is what freedom is, then what is rebellion? Louise is not sure. She thinks for a moment and says that she recognizes that maybe she has not been free, that a lot of her freedom is an attempt to rebel against her mother. She quickly turns to me. How can I be free, goddamnit? Tell me. I tell Louise that I cannot tell anyone how to be free, but I can help her to discover how she is not free, to be *aware* of how she is still caught up with her need to do just the opposite of what would please her mother and that she has settled for that instead of finding her own freedom. Louise presses me. That is not enough for her; how can she be free? I tell her that just as I would not let her coerce me into not making a small lecture when I thought it would be useful to Doug, so I will not let her coerce me into pontificating on how to be free. I suggest that if I were to give her a prescription, she would only do the opposite. I then repeat that I think the best thing I can do for Louise is to help her become aware of where she is now, of how she is living her life. Once she is clear about this she can go on to explore her freedom and make it valid for herself, not a parody of her mother's values.

Louise is somewhat mollified and doesn't answer. I gently try to indicate that if I replace her mother as someone who gives her blueprints on how to live, little will have been accomplished for her. Perhaps Louise can grasp in our encounter this evening that she has tried to force me into positions so that she could rebel against them. Maybe this is something to be aware of as a beginning. Louise is torn. She accepts what I have said, but she still wants more. I indicate that she will have to live with this for the time being, that this is all I have to offer her at this moment, that our group time is up and that I am tired.

So we have the formal ending of the group. When a group is young, when it has just started to meet, I invite members each to say a few words about how they felt about what happened. This gives shy members a chance to speak. However, when the group is not new, then members feel free to express themselves during the course of the session and they request that we abandon the "roundup." I do, however, ask Doug if he wants to say anything, since he is new, even if the group is not. He smiles and answers that he feels less frightened, but he is still not sure about how open he can be. Others state that he will have time, that Richard, Harry and Louise have been members for a year.

The group is over. We have spent between two and three

hours, intensely involved in one another's intimate thoughts and feelings, experimented with meanings, attitudes, behaviors. We have tried to be direct, honest, open. And now it is finished. But only by the clock. Often, group members are unwilling to part simply because the session is over. The session may be completed, but they are not finished. So they linger as I collect coffee cups and empty ashtrays. Some help me; others embrace one another, laugh, talk; some slink away, eager to disappear, for the experience of a group can be very powerful and for some people it offers more powerful contact with others, the world, than they have had all week, and so they search for the quiet of the cave. I have no rules about the cleanup. It is my office; I do not feel burdened if no help is forthcoming. I am not grateful if I have a volunteer. Sometimes, if the session has been particularly moving, I have difficulty getting members to leave. I shoo them out in mock anger: It is late and I am tired. Usually some of them will walk around the corner to a bar, have a drink and continue talking. Or they may stand on the street in front of the office, deciding who will give whom a ride, who wants a snack, or just chatting.

I have no rules about group members socializing between meetings, though many therapists do. Some members become friends or lovers. If the friends fight or if the lovers quarrel, then I ask that the arguments do not become the pretext to quit the group but that these fights be brought back into the group for "work."

Just as members will meet for dinner or a snack before the beginning of the group and then bring into the group session the rivalries, jealousies and hurt feelings that develop, so they are free to meet after the session and continue the group without me. Sometimes, regardless of whether or not I want to know it, members are inhibited by my presence, and in a bar or at an early snack they feel freer to develop warm feelings without what they regard as my parental eye. When they want to, they can bring to the group what happens in the bar after the sessions, and again at times this is very useful. But I ordinarily never ask what happens before or after the group sessions at these pre- or post-meetings. I want group members to have the right to their own lives without my having to impose on them the necessity of reporting everything to me. One of the dangers of being a therapist is to believe I must know everything that is important in someone's life. I don't want to be their gestapo, insisting on knowing all. I have quite enough to deal with in what happens in the individual and private sessions without having to snoop. I want people to be responsible for their own lives when I am not there, and so when I go on vacation I invite each group to continue meeting in my absence, if they wish. It is their decision. I prefer that they be clear that they can exist without me, even in a group session, and that what they make of their lives outside of sessions is something I am interested in but will not pry into.

Finally all the members have gone. I take a last look at the room, note that it is reasonably neat, that the ashtrays and coffee cups have been removed, turn out the light and close the door until the next day.

The group is over, but I still have not discussed "work" and what it is. During the session we all worked, but especially Harry, Richard, Doug and Louise. To some therapists, these four members of the group sat in the "hot seat." The "hot seat" is a term Fritz Perls invented to characterize one form of group therapy as he practiced it. Primarily Fritz (almost no one called him Dr. Perls or Friedrich) worked with one person at a time, with the other group members as audience. The person he worked with received his exclusive attention and was therefore in the "hot seat."

In my groups I prefer a much higher level of participation from the other members, so that in a sense the group as a whole or individual members in addition to myself act as therapist. In this way we all get some of the action, and the therapist role is not so sacrosanct or exclusively mine.

When Harry, Richard, Doug or Louise agree to work, whether

verbally or non-verbally, they accept the full focus of the group's attention. They accept the need to take directions, to try new experiments, to listen to others, often in spite of what their common sense tells them.

As they work they are often aware of a wide range of feelings and conditions. They can't hear too well, they misunderstand what is being said, they become easily distracted, they feel humiliated, they just want to crawl away, they can't sense how they are presenting their thoughts and feelings, they are sure that no one is interested, that people are bored and want them to stop, that people are criticizing them and so on and on and on.

In other words, when group members work, they resist in myriad ways. Perls says the patient has a right to resist, and this is part of his work. It is part of my work and the work of the group to point out not only that he is resisting but also how he resists. If he becomes aware of how he resists, then he can do something about it. If he becomes aware of his defense and what he gets out of it, then he can think about whether he wants to continue using it in the same way.

Defenses and resistances are basically valuable parts of a person's makeup that may become rigid or overused. Harry's feelings of weakness permit him to avoid facing his strengths, which he feels must challenge his father; Louise's need for rebellion keeps her from finding out what she really wants and from dealing with facing up to her feelings about her mother. As a person "works" in group, he can explore his defenses and resistances. He can also explore new ways of meeting situations. Many of the *ad hoc* experiments in which Richard and Harry role-play are designed so that new elements can emerge as well as the opportunity to see old patterns more clearly. Work then becomes an adventure in truly getting to know yourself better, in trying out new ways of being, in coming closer to accepting yourself right here and now—not as you wish you'd like to be, not as you fear others see you, but as you are.

The focus shifts rapidly, if I am willing to let it, from Harry to

Richard, then in a more formal way to Doug and then quickly to Louise. I have to be willing to "flow" with a group, to give up a good deal of my control, to give up my ideas of what ought to happen and what ought not to happen. Many therapists are afraid of groups for this reason. They don't feel comfortable being that loose with a group, to go with it where it wants to go. I do not mean that I will go anywhere with a group. When I think or feel that something important is being avoided or deliberately ignored, I feel free to intervene. I am very active in my groups, but I also try to be very responsive to where others want to go, to pay attention to what they think is important, to trust that something useful will emerge if I am willing to go with someone else's idea, and if we end up in a blind alley, then at least we tried. I don't always have to win or find victory. Sometimes in a group we can struggle all evening and what we have at the end is a better appreciation of how much an individual wants to stay where he is. This is something to respect and to experience.

What I prefer is that the group session develop a life of its own, its own momentum, and that each session have its own unique form. No two groups will be alike. In this way we have the best opportunity of not making work boring. But sometimes it will be tedious. When a person is well defended and unwilling to risk much, then the group or I can become impatient. At that point we are free to go on to something or someone else or to try to stay with the person's resistance and see if we can loosen his block, see if we can accept that this is where he is now, and if it is good enough for him, then it is good enough for us. For some, working in group is such a threat that they prefer not to take the risk.

Working can be considered a test, a performance, a chance to gain insight, to get through something, to be the center of attention. With a group working at its best, "work" often shifts in an easy, relaxed manner among several members in rapid fashion. However, the group is not always that relaxed, and more typically one member has his time to work. Some group members generate enormous tension when they have an opportunity to work, and despite all of my efforts and the efforts of the other members of the group, we are foiled. The threat of exposing anything to the rest of us becomes immobilizing, and that is that. I have had members of the group attend regularly and largely sit silent, regardless of what is happening. When they personally are asked if they will work on anything, there may be a grudging agreement, and that is about all that is forthcoming. And yet these members with their stubborn strength, their ability to withhold and say no, no matter what pressure, will stick with the group and gain from it but not because of their active, direct participation. They successfully resist learning how to open up to others while the group is ongoing, but then outside, in their private lives, they take advantage of what they will not share with the rest of us.

7 . The Group and Me

I cannot emphasize too strongly how important and vital the group is. In the preceding chapter I have given a brief description of what goes on in a group, and I have tried to show why the group is so useful. But I haven't managed to get across how the group is organized, how the members interact, what happens in a group. Here I would like to take the group from a different perspective and discuss each of its three major parts: the therapist, the member who works and the others in the group.

1. *The therapist.* I have a problem in running a group that is more acute than in private sessions. Private sessions of two persons can rely on a conversational mode, a back and forth between two people. Question and answer, statement and counter-statement. Of course, I still have the issue of how much to say, of how much to intervene. But I know that if I don't do it, then either you will have to do it or it will be left undone. With the group, there is the additional chance that if I keep silent, someone in the group will intervene and move the situation along a therapeutic dimension. (There is also the equal opportunity that a group member will intervene and move the situation toward a non-therapeutic goal, but we can discuss that later.)

In a group I prefer to say as little as possible. The aim is to have all of the group members function as therapists to themselves. Unfortunately that is not always possible, or even if it were, then why would I be needed at all? Why not have a leaderless group? And why not? This is precisely what happened with a group of my trainees in therapy. After two to three years of a colloquium they were sufficiently confident of their own abilities so that they now meet on a regular basis without me.

In similar fashion, when I leave town and cannot attend a group session, I suggest the group meet without me. This is the most striking evidence that they can survive without me. It is also important for the group to recognize that when I am not there they can proceed with work and get results.

Still, for my own sake, I have to believe that I have something to contribute to the group. First I provide an atmosphere that states that we have come together to try to find new ways of living, with ourselves and others. I offer an opportunity in the presence of others to try to do things that have been difficult if not impossible up to that moment. At its most extreme, for some people just to speak up in a group and expect to be heard is a new experience. Just recently in one of my groups a man of about forty who had been a member for more than a year spoke up for the first time. Previously he had resisted tenaciously almost all attempts to get him to relax, to speak his mind, to work on his problems. The group had suffered, and I along with them, as we tried to extract feelings, thoughts, problems from him. If we ignored him he was content. If we didn't ignore him, then he was largely like a turtle or a rock. If we asked him to glory in being a rock, he was contemptuous. But gradually, during this period, he took small steps, infinitesimal steps, excruciatingly tiny steps that it was possible to belittle or ignore. And then it happened. He arrived at the group and selected the most powerful group member for attack. Very calmly he took aim and selected defects in his character. My silent man was now verbally angry, brutal, without mercy. The stronger member could well afford to accept the attack and had something to learn from the silent man. The rest of us, the group and I included, enjoyed the demonstration of what lay beneath the silence: a desire to be powerful and controlling that our silent man was now willing to risk and to attain. Laughingly I said that I expected to be attacked in another six weeks, but I was wrong. For once the strongest group member was disposed of, it was my turn to be attacked verbally. And this came in two minutes.

Now the experience I have just mentioned was just as powerful as when Eliza Doolittle first enunciates "The rain in Spain falls mainly in the plain," to the astonished pleasure of Professor Higgins and Colonel Pickering. We had all witnessed a minor miracle. Someone who had been blocked, limited, stunted, had just taken a giant step toward attaining a new level of growth and development. And the excitement for me and all of the members of the group was that we had had a part in it and had been privileged to be witnesses to the event.

My own contribution had been in part to offer a kind of hope and faith that this kind of change was possible, to create an atmosphere that promoted taking small steps toward change that were free of shame, fear, guilt, humiliation, degradation. And then to have contributed experiments for the person to take.

The experiments are vital toward helping someone contact important parts of himself that he uses to block his attempts to change. In suggesting experiments I try particularly hard to be alive and inventive, to respond to the needs of this particular individual at this particular moment.

At one point I thought of listing a series of experiments as a part of this book, but I rejected that because they would then be "cold," and the value of an experiment is that it is something "hot" that is cooked up especially for that moment. This is not to say that some experiments cannot be transmitted, but I would rather not offer this kind of encyclopedia. In creating experiments I continually surprise myself. By keeping alive to the situation at the moment, I am inspired to create an experiment that was not there before. In this fashion, in the group, I function somewhat as a magician. I take elements that are already there but I transmute them. This can sometimes be frightening to group members who have a large investment in the banal or the ordinary. Recently when one group member was blocked about what she wanted to work on, I asked her to tell each of us one of the things she didn't want to work on. Here I was following an established Gestalt practice of going with an individual's resistance rather than fighting it. It was designed to elicit something new and fresh by staying with what the person was trying to avoid at the moment, what he wanted to work on. She quickly said she didn't want to work on doors, chairs, windows, lava, tables, floors. *Lava*—now where did that come from? The young lady was very gentle, quiet, subdued. I asked her to "be lava," and she complied by improvising a lovely dance that built in a crescendo, an eruption, and then slowly subsided. All of us were astonished by the beauty, intelligence and most of all the emotion of the dance that had issued from this blocked woman. This was a fairly new group and one of the members said she found me frightening and weird. What would I do next? I was undependable. What she wanted was something safe and sheltered. She would have preferred tables, chairs, doors but not windows, certainly not lava.

I have another important function in the group: to put the lid back on. During a good part of the group sessions I try to keep situations moving, to keep people alive to possibilities, to help explore new areas or blocked passages. Sometimes—not too often but sometimes—people tend to get carried along by the powerful new emotions or powerful old emotions, and then I have to step in. I am speaking particularly about fights and crying.

When I first started to run groups I was afraid of violence. I didn't want "fighting groups," as they are sometimes called, when a therapist deliberately encourages people to be verbally and even physically violent. I still am not completely comfortable with a lot of hostility being thrown about, but as time has passed I have learned to deal with some of my own fears. Still, when people actually start fighting, as they do occasionally, then I try to stay with the battle until I feel that it is no longer useful to the people involved. When a fight begins, the other group members quickly clear a space so that no pointed edges or heavy objects are in the immediate vicinity of the combatants. They also quickly remove eyeglasses from the combatants and stand ready to disengage them should it be necessary. At a point when I have determined that there is little more therapeutically to be gained from a battle, I ask the combatants to stop and they pretty much stop. They are not after blood or final destruction. Then we can talk or not talk about what happened, depending on the situation.

What is terribly important, though, is that just as I can take the lid off, so I can put the lid back on, when it is necessary. This is just as important when tears become overwhelming, when an individual in the group lets go and sobs and sobs and sobs. Once again some of the group members can be frightened. Tears for some members are much more precious than gold; they cry only in the most extreme situations. I have always felt more comfortable with tears than extreme anger, and so I have been more relaxed about comforting people who cry. And just as I would hold someone in "real life" who was sobbing, so I do not hesitate to do the same in the group. Here again I make a decision. When a person permits himself to open old wounds and pour out his tears, he is having an important experience. I do not try to cut it short because it is embarrassing to watch. Similarly, it is important for other members of the group to learn that they can comfort others in their fear or grief, so I permit them to comfort others. If, however, I think that the individual sobbing is particularly distressed, then I may comfort him myself or encourage several group members to hold the person. Some of my own most important moments as a member of a group have taken place when I learned I could get very angry and I would not go crazy and when I cried and cried about ancient pieces of the past, like my mother's death, which I had thought were so nicely put away. I would not like to deny similar opportunities to others.

Boredom presents a special problem in the group. I can't say that I am never bored, but the experience is different for me. If someone is being particularly resistant, then many members of the group are likely to become bored and to turn off. If I am working hard with someone who is resisting, then I am much more likely to become angry. Thus I may lose contact with the rest of the group at that moment.

I also have a different appreciation of boredom. From a Gestalt Therapy point of view, boredom is a signal: The bored person is withholding another emotion. He wants something else to happen, but he is not willing to take responsibility for it. The typical example is a person talking to someone and feeling bored. If we examine his boredom, we discover that he really wants either to tell the "bore" to shut up or else to run and escape the bore. But his good manners tell him to stay there and take it. Someone's boredom is an important piece of information, an opportunity for him to learn that he wants something to change. Now when I am working with someone who is resistant, I am so engaged in trying to find a path from his being stuck that I often have little time to be bored. However, that is not the experience of the rest of the group. They feel quite free to express their boredom or else take the consequences. If they are too polite to say, I am bored, or You are boring me, then they can expect to remain bored. If something more important than their boredom is at stake, then we will come to that. But if someone is just trying to bore others as a security measure, to stop anything further from happening, then we can either agree and stop or else examine the technique of boredom to keep people at bay.

When someone is deliberately trying to bore me as a means of stopping something from developing that is alive, I have trouble in not getting abrupt and short. My own passion is that since we are gathered to do therapy, a person should try. Later I can reason with myself that at times it is even more important for a person to resist therapy and say, No, thank you, I don't want any. This can be a valuable means for a person to see that he is in charge of his own life; he can have therapy or not have therapy; he can resist therapy or try to go along with it. No one is making him a victim, no one is forcing him to do what he doesn't want to. In other words, he is responsible for his own life.

What else do I offer the group? I act as a kind of elder statesman, a resident oracle, a chief magician. When the group is stuck, they can turn to me and see what I can come up with.

As I said earlier, I prefer that the members of the group take charge and run it themselves. But since I have more experience in groups (I must have spent more than 6,000 hours in groups by now), both as a therapist and as a group member, and since I have greater training in Gestalt Therapy, and since I am older than 90 percent of the group members, and since they have specifically selected me as their group therapist, then it seems likely that in a pinch I will come up with something to keep the show going. Now *show* is a good word to use, for there is a great sense of theater in an exciting group session. What is to me a never-ending source of wonder, pride and glory is that if I have spent more than 6,000 hours in groups, my experience is that no two of them are ever the same. Not only do the group members change, not only do I change as I grow (or diminish) as a therapist, but even the same experiment is different when used with a different group or a different individual.

As I said earlier, I try not to use canned experiments, but there are some uniformities. I cannot be so original that I can completely invent a totally new system at each group. I rely on certain kinds of lead-ins at the beginning of working with an individual when he is resisting. They seem tedious at times, but I consider them similar to any kind of necessary preparation: A dramatist has to get his characters on stage and let the audience know where they are and how they relate to one another, regardless of what the stage action will be; a cook must set the table, no matter what the menu is. And though I deplore this introduction, some of the group members learn the technique and take over for me. They do this not just for my benefit, although I am grateful not to have to lead a person past his initial resistance, but so that they gain facility for working with themselves. They learn the first easy stages of resistance and how to counteract them, how to lead beyond them, so that they can do their own work, with themselves.

And finally I close the group. Or better, I call a halt to the formal therapy session. When I was younger and had the energy, when I had only a vague sense of my limitations, I would work with a group for three, four, five hours, and the rest of the group would stay with me, excited, tired, exhausted. Many complained that we worked so late, at such a pitch, that they were too wound up to sleep that night. So I call a halt to the group. As I pointed out in the preceding chapter, the group need not end there, only the therapy.

2. *The group member who works.* There is no formal arrangement whereby only one person works or any limit to how long he works. Some evenings, when group members are open and relaxed, as many as eight people have worked in a single session. The focus of interest shifts rapidly as each person is attended to. Sometimes two people work, or one person starts to work and another joins in, presumably to help or to hinder him, and the focus shifts to the second member. But usually what happens is that an individual presents a problem that he wants to work on, and the group and I respond.

If the individual is sincere in his effort to work, he will feel a good deal of excitement and some anxiety. He has the full attention of a dozen people, all intent on helping him in any way possible. If he is not sincere in his attempt to work, then he will likely not feel the excitement and anxiety. Instead, he will seek to control or manipulate the group so that he can claim he has tried to get something and then reluctantly conclude that it was not possible. When this happens the group eventually catches on and then considerable anger is expressed. Why did you waste our time? If you didn't want to work, why not just sit there? I had wanted to work and now there isn't time. But despite the anger of the group, it is still important to members to resist in this fashion. Indeed, for him for whom it is necessary to push people away by passive provocation, to manipulate for control and then to lose it and feel guilty and ashamed, for this person the group affords an opportunity to create this situation in a controlled setting and to experience it keenly.

If the person wants to work and feels excited and anxious, then he is also likely to experience difficulty in concentrating. One problem in working is that a person runs the risk of getting flooded. Too much excitement is something that not many of us are used to dealing with. In such instances there is a tendency for a person to shut down; or to become the tool of the group, passively agreeing with whatever is offered; or to become confused and not know what is happening in any precise kind of way; or to become hostile as a means of stopping anything further from happening. So it becomes another place for collaboration between myself, the group and the individual who is working. We, the group and I, have to keep up the investigation so that we can go further. At the same time I have to be responsive to whether or not the individual is able to go ahead in a meaningful manner. If I become convinced that the individual needs a rest, a breathing space, then I do not hesitate to interrupt and to slow down the action. Even so, once excitement has reached a certain stage, it becomes difficult for the individual to maintain good contact with himself. And here is one of the many signs of the potency of the group. I do not expect an individual to absorb everything that has taken place that evening. Or the next day. Or the next week. Sometimes what happens in a group is so pertinent to the person working that he spends the next several days or even weeks assimilating it, chewing it over, absorbing it into a part of himself that he is comfortable with. Sometimes the assimilation goes on much longer. I recently received a letter from a former group member asserting that he was still digesting his group experiences of several years before.

A kind of informal rule develops about a person working, what I learned as a graduate student to call *moeurs*. Someone who works honestly has put himself on the line; he has tried to be open, to expose himself, to take in what is offered, to go along with experiments, interpretations, observations. He becomes at that moment a hero who has faced his own demons and the demon of the group as well. For that reason group members offer him respect, and people acquire reputations as to their ability to work in group. New members are particularly impressed with the ability of the old hands, the pros, to open up in group. Part of the motive for risking all of the excitement and anxiety of working in the group comes from another *moeur*. The group develops the point of view that each person should have a turn, each person should submit to working. I, in my Olympian way, take the position that a person is free to work or not as he chooses, is free to attend group and not work if he is too frightened or delays for some other reason. And that is all very well for me, but within the group there is a different viewpoint. We are all here to get on with it, and if we are willing to plunge into the cold bath, then if you are going to be one with us, you have to do it too. Thus, despite the group's apparent sophistication in understanding others, at the same time it adheres to primitive ethics that are not so sensitive. Frankly, except in special cases when a particular person is genuinely so frightened of working that I deem it wise to interfere and protect him from what he cannot manage at a certain stage, I avoid dealing with this *moeur*. Here is one place where I most often, but not always, am willing to accept the authority of the group to find its own way, even though I may not thereby gain the respect of the ACLU.

In some ways the person who works in the group has a more intense experience than in individual therapy. He has more time, sometimes as much as two or three hours, and much more attention from a dozen others. He often experiences a kind of emotional bloodbath, crying, shouting, depression, helplessness, a sense of power. At the conclusion of working there occurs a kind of catharsis that the individual almost always experiences pleasurably. He feels spent, he feels purged, he has let it all hang out. He shows a kind of glow and radiance. It is not at all unlikely for me to see quite clearly vast changes in a person's looks after he has worked. His face is calmer, his body seems much more relaxed, his breathing is better, his posture straighter.

I want to be clear that these immediate gains are momentarily wonderful and usually short-lived. One of the dangers of the newer therapies is that they are able to stimulate people, and often the therapist and the patient decide that these short-term effects constitute therapy. Fritz Perls was particularly contemptuous of what he termed the "turner-oners," the therapists who stimulated patients and offered little else. Thus, it is important to be aware, to recognize that in the group the person working may be bathed in a wonderful glow after he has worked, or even as he worked, but that this rush of good feeling is not the same as having been able to continue to work with difficult material that is now uncovered or available for mastery week after week. In a weekend workshop there is no follow-up on what happens to a person and no means of helping him to integrate what has happened in the group but that is not finished at the end of the session. For this reason I want the continuity of weekly sessions, even if they are not so dramatic as a flying circus, as one of the turner-oners calls his therapeutic menagerie. I would be very unhappy about letting the whole event languish because it was just a weekend workshop after all, and what you got you got, and that's it.

I have kept repeating that the group experience can be very exciting and dramatic. Let me try to illustrate this by offering a few snapshots of what can happen:

A man says he feels weak, impotent. He cannot influence anyone. I ask him to lift me. He fears he cannot. I offer my trust, and he does so gingerly. I point out that he was afraid to know his own strength and suggest that he lift me again and carry me around the room. He does so with gusto. We both enjoy the experience. He becomes very excited.

A man lives a meager, narrow social life. He has wit, a good income, good health, but he is over fifty years old and homosexual. I encourage him to approach each group member and tell them with sincerity that he is old, lonely and homosexual. Each member is free to demand that he repeat it again if they do not feel the honesty of his remark. I ask him to repeat it three times, and he bursts into tears. (The next week he begins to widen his experiences, and he feels tremendous. Six months later he is leading an active social life and beginning to have a fuller sex life.)

A similar setting. A man is ashamed of being Mexican. I ask him to approach each group member, who asks him, "Who are you?" He responds, "I am Luis, and I am a Mexican." Luis is flattered by the experience, but there is no happy ending. Later he will go to live in Scotland for a year, and just as formerly he had told people he was Spanish, he now develops an English accent. But we tried.

A recently divorced woman is afraid of meeting new men. They will not approve of her. She is no longer attractive. We improvise a party. She sits next to the group member she finds most attractive, and we see what develops. Later we ask the partners to reverse roles, and she plays the attractive man and he plays her. The situation is very painful for her. (Later she learns how to meet men, and now she is ready to approach her own difficulties in keeping them.)

A woman expressed her fear of losing her job in advertising. She has to be creative about selling toilet paper on TV. She is pre-ulcerous, and she has had an ulcer in the past. A new ad campaign is about to be launched, and she must come up with a blitz ad. The group intervenes and offers feedback on advertising and its position in the world. Our friend had felt she must be a success, must accept advertising on its own terms. As a result of the group, she gains perspective on the career she has chosen, begins to operate differently in her agency, and her stomach problems begin to subside.

A young man feels dead. He can recognize issues only with his mind. We ask him to play dead. We lay him out. We have a mock funeral service. He is asked to deliver his own eulogy. He can feel his own death keenly!

A drug addict takes pills to numb himself from his intense feelings. He is afraid that if he expresses his feelings he will go crazy. We invite him to go crazy. He lets go, screams, hollers, bangs his feet, has a good rage, a real tantrum. And then calms down. He is not crazy and is not in danger of going crazy. If he still takes pills, it is for other reasons, and we are free to pursue these at another time.

Husband and wife are in the group together. They are thinking of separating. Each is engaged in affairs with others. But they are very polite to each other. They never quarrel. I invite them to quarrel now, in the group. They have great difficulty, but they manage. Then they really get into it. Now they realize they have been withholding a good many feelings from each other, and perhaps their looking for other sexual partners is a way of being angry in an indirect way.

A young woman is newly divorced but is unable to get used to the idea that her settlement included the house. She claims to want nothing more than to be rid of her husband haunting her home. I ask her to tell us all of the reasons why she wants to be haunted by him, and out pours a whole host of reasons that indicate that she is still unfinished with her divorce, that she still has much to attend to before she can take possession of her own life.

An attractive young woman has hidden her own sexual feelings from herself and her husband. I ask her not to wait to be courted by the men in the group but to go to each and be seductive. At first she is very embarrassed and ashamed, but as she proceeds she begins to enjoy herself and feel freer, much to the pleasure of the men in the group.

A middle-aged man is lonely and unhappy, yet distrustful and rejecting of any help. The group members try to offer him interest, care, support, but he ignores them. I ask each group member to offer him something that is particularly tempting for him, but he is to refuse the gift. By deliberately focusing on his refusal he comes to a better appreciation of how he has become lonely, how he holds himself back.

A young woman suffers from migraine. She has had them since she was six years old, and her mother had them. She believes they are mainly neurological, inherited. During one group session she begins to have a migraine. I challenge her, tell her I will take away her headache. I ask her to be angry with me. She manages to fly into a rage, and presto, her migraine has disappeared!

A young man has not seen his parents in five years. When they last saw him he had shoulder-length hair, a beard, and he took drugs. Now he is clean-cut and uses only pot, but they know nothing of his change, and they are still estranged. He weeps because Christmas is coming and he is lonely, but he feels unwanted in his family. I ask him to pretend to call his home and speak to his father. Reluctantly he does so but finds that his "father" is more accepting than he had hoped. Later that night after leaving the group he does in fact call his father. His father is very warm and sends him air fare home to the West Coast. He is radiant.

A young man has spent years in therapy, trying to overcome his early training to be neat, careful, polite. He has overlearned his lesson. In the group I ask him to be naughty and destroy something. He selects an old Victorian pillow and rips it apart with great gusto. Feathers fill the room so that we are all covered. He is filled with glee and more willing to respond to his impulses.

A young woman had a child when she was an adolescent and has spent most of her adult life trying to be a mother and yet have a life of her own. Now she is pregnant by her current boyfriend and wonders if she should have a child. She states strongly that she does not want one. I encourage her to build a case both for having an abortion and not having an abortion. She discovers that she has very strong feelings about wanting to have a child again. She weeps and weeps and is comforted by other women in the group, married and unmarried, who also share with her (and us) their own experiences with abortions. She has not reached a decision, but she feels better, regardless of what her eventual choice will be.

Two members of the group are angry with each other. Both have difficulty expressing anger. Each is musical. I invite them to improvise an operatic aria and sing their feelings to each other. Each accepts the challenge. They do a beautiful job both of singing and of saying what is on their mind.

A young lesbian is in exile from her proper family in New England. She fears their disapproval, particularly the Ladies'

Garden Club members who are close to her mother. She claims to detest them. I ask her to be one of the members of the Ladies' Garden Club, the most hated one, and to converse with her. She finds that the woman is not such an ogre and that she is not so frightened of her.

A young Italian woman has been raised puritanically. She has been taught that men are superior and women are to serve them. Yet she deeply resents this point of view. She experiences difficulty in working with men. I ask her to become the most extreme representative of Women's Liberation and to address her current boss, who she feels demeans her. She speechifies energetically and reports next week that she feels more confident at work, better able to deal with her boss.

A middle-aged man's mother is dying. He reports no feelings toward her beyond a desire to inherit her small capital. All of the other members of the group have mothers who are living. I ask each to imagine his own mother's death. Some members weep when they do so. All but one can recognize how emotionally laden such an event would be. The middle-aged man is willing to consider that maybe he has some feelings he is not willing to consider. Later, once she has indeed died, he reports defiantly that he still feels nothing but the lifting of a burden. He also notes that the most feeling he had was when a friend of his mother wrote him a sympathy note. I ask him to tell us what it contained. He repeats it as best he can and begins to become aware of the grief he has hidden. He starts to cry and the group comforts him.

A young woman has been ringed by death—her brother, her sister, her father. Now a member of her ski lodge died on the slopes. She comes to group and asks nothing. I notice her upset face and ask her what the trouble is. She tells us of this latest death and collapses in sobbing. The women in the group cradle her like a baby, hug her and rock her. She puts her head on the bosom of the largest woman and receives comfort.

A middle-aged man is lonely, unable to connect socially or sexually with any partners at all. Presumably his life is filled with success: a thriving business, lots of publicity, invitations by all the right people to all the right parties. I ask him to invent a blues song for himself and sing it. He quickly produces a moving series of couplets, describing his empty and lonely life. Later during the week he sings parts to himself and for the first time invites a friend to dinner.

Not all of the experiments are successful, but as in any true experiment it is possible to learn something. Nor are we finished when the experiments succeed in helping a person to take a step. He is no longer stuck, no longer fixed in a rigid posture that hinders his growth. Now we can proceed to the next step and after that the next. The valuable opportunity the group affords the person who is working is the chance to take those areas where he is experiencing the greatest difficulty and in a protected, safe atmosphere to take risks and see what happens. In all of the above experiments I could not have predicted what would take place, granted that the individual agreed to try to perform the experiment honestly. I of course had some notions and certainly I proposed each experiment based on these notions, but what I had not predicted was often at least as important as what I had predicted.

3. *The other members of the group.* Obviously the person who works in the group is the one who stands to gain the most. However, the other members of the group also participate and benefit in a variety of ways. For example, many members are often very frightened of the experiments, of the prospect of standing openly before the group and exposing themselves. When they see other members work they often gain courage to

confront their own difficulties. Often when someone is working in the group other members will nod in a special manner that indicates their own identification with the worker's difficulties. Sometimes I will seek eye contact with group members whose situations are particularly similar to that being worked on, and the person will send back the message that he is only too aware of how close he feels to what is happening.

The atmosphere of the group is not always so charged with intense feelings. Sometimes we all laugh and joke and the climate becomes quite playful. Here too the group members have an opportunity to learn that despite all their difficulties, life need not be so grim. Some group members feel that their neurosis entitles them to make a career of feeling sorry for themselves and being glum. The occasional playful, party atmosphere of the group serves as a healthy antidote to overserious attention to suffering.

When the experiment involves role-playing, sometimes I ask the worker to select someone to be his wife, mother, girlfriend. The person selected then has an opportunity not only to be helpful to his fellow group member but to explore his own feelings as he plays someone of a different age, sex or relationship.

Some members of the group refuse to participate. They continue to come to group but not to take part. They never volunteer to work; they do so only under great pressure and then only minimally, so that I come to let them be. They offer almost nothing to other members of the group who do work. These silent ones obviously engender great hostility from the other members of the group, who consider them parasites, freeloaders. Often other members of the group invite them to leave. My own experience is that these individuals, who as you might gather have strong negative feelings and who are also strong on spite, nonetheless take a great deal from the group. They don't give the group much, but at least they can come to see how stingy they are and how this affects others. With time, years even, these silent members of the group slowly, slowly melt, change. But this does not mean that they are willing to share these changes with the other members of the group. This information, which I receive in a variety of ways, is carefully kept hidden from the other members of the group. Although these silent members often do come to deal with life in a more satisfactory manner, they never resolve their relations with the group, and after they leave they take with them their secret, stingy ways of coping with others.

Those members who do participate have an opportunity to express a wide range of feelings, good and bad, in an accepting atmosphere, and often warm, tender mutual feelings develop. Some of these feelings result in genuine friendships that persist long after members cease to belong to the group. Indeed, even marriages have taken place among group members, though so far not among my own. But who knows, just this week two ex-members of the group went away on a weekend together, and two current members went off to meet each other's parents. Maybe here I have some of my own fantasies to attend to.

8 . The Value of Group and Individual Therapy

Many people wonder, Isn't it enough to have just individual therapy? What is the use of group therapy? How is it different from individual therapy? Isn't it just more of the same, only more embarrassing with all those strangers? For me group and individual therapy are not two opposed forms of therapy, but when integrated they form a continuum of treatment, each offering its own sources for helping a person to grow and develop.

We can begin by noting the similarities between group and individual therapy, and then, using those as background, we can go on to differentiate each form. I would like to point out that my own preferred method of working is first to enroll an individual in private therapy and then, after we have established a feeling for each other, invite him to join a group. Please note the word *invite*.

Most people who come for therapy have difficulty with relationships with others. Often they avoid others, singly or in groups. If they are willing to risk starting therapy, why, they can tell themselves that the therapist is kindly, knows what he is doing, has their interests at heart and at bottom they are paying him, and he is only one person whom they have to control. A group is much more threatening to each of these assumptions. Many people are very frightened about joining a group, and we often talk about this for some time before a person agrees to attend a group session. Since the group experience can be so powerful and threatening, I ask anyone who is thinking of joining the group to attend at least four sessions before he decides whether or not he wants to remain in the group.

Some people point-blank refuse to join a group. They give all kinds of reasons for this, but usually they are just too frightened. For some who do, the first couple of months are filled with terror as each group meeting approaches. Later many become devoted to the group, and for some it is more valuable than individual sessions.

Some people particularly want the experience of being in a group. They may seek me out because they have heard that I have several groups and believe strongly in the efficacy of the group. Once a person has joined a group, I have the advantage of working with him in two different settings, and the person has the advantage of three or four hours of therapy per week instead of just fifty minutes with me.

A person usually enters therapy because he is having more difficulty than he believes is his due and he doesn't know what to do about it. (If he did, why then he would save the time and expense and do it himself.) When he comes for a consultation, he has an opportunity to size me up, to see if he likes me and, perhaps more important, to make a judgment about whether he thinks I can really help him. For this reason I make a special effort in a consultation to reach out to this new person, to take a risk, to go out on a limb to try to offer him something, so that he can feel a little relieved when he leaves, so that he can believe that maybe something can happen for him and that someone will try to be there for him. Usually this is not difficult to do, since a person usually presents more of himself in a consultation. He has not had an opportunity to develop means of resistance other than those provided by his own nature.

The person entering therapy usually has some fantasies of who he will be when we have finished our work and how it will all happen. But gradually he becomes aware that he can look forward to my support, to gaining insights, sometimes with my aid and sometimes without, occasionally an interpretation and occasionally some clarification. (Yes, I know Gestalt therapists are *not* supposed to offer interpretations, but just take the trouble to read Fritz Perls' work carefully and then judge for yourself. Those who categorically state Gestalt therapists do not offer interpretations are probably as guilty of introjecting concepts they have not digested as are the Freudians who can never interrupt an association.)

Now depending on our work, a person will arrive at a greater awareness of himself and his needs, will be willing to take responsibility for his own actions and to take risks in working out new possibilities and arrangements for his life. All of this is possible in both individual and group therapy, but the constellations are different.

In individual therapy, the cast is limited to the two of us, just you and me. Our relationship is free to become as intense as we want to make it. One of the dangers is that it will become more intense than we might like, and if this develops, then we will have to attend to it.

Within individual therapy, when I suggest an experiment, then despite your reluctance to embarrass yourself, I am the only member of the audience. Once you begin to trust me, you may feel free without too much embarrassment to try it and see what emerges.

In group therapy, the cast includes a dozen different types. Our cozy relationship is rent asunder. You and I not only have to deal with each other but a wide range of personalities. You may appeal to me with your frightened eyes or a wistful smile, but if you try to ask me to protect you directly, the group will not allow it. As for me, all the polite ways you tried to insinuate yourself with me become more transparent, when I have an opportunity to see you behave more spontaneously with the other members of the group, more as you do in everyday life without so much editing to impress me.

One of the main differences between group and individual therapy lies in the level of excitement. A dozen people are less likely than I might be to sit politely and permit you to resist confronting your problems. You might have learned how to manage me, but it is unlikely you will be able to figure out how to manipulate all of us. With a dozen people listening intently, reacting strongly, an atmosphere can develop that is sometimes like that of a good party, or an exciting theater performance, or a moving talk between friends, or a playful encounter, and so on. Usually our private session is a little more staid. We are less likely to be led astray from your concerns by my own preoccupations, and so more time is saved. But in a group you have the support of a dozen persons, each of whom is willing to expend energy on your behalf as you struggle with a difficult time. When a group is "hot," when there is no bullshit and they are right on target—I am deliberately trying to include all the clichés—then it is a wondrous sight to behold and a marvelous thing to hear. When a good group breaks up, at ten or so, and after they have gone off to have a drink for an hour or more, then by midnight they are still full of energy and so up from what has happened that they find it difficult to let go of all that excitement.

Ah, there is yet another difference between group and individual therapy and one to which I am not a party. Once the group session is over, members are free to meet or avoid other members, as they wish.

Many therapists either discourage or forbid these gatherings where a good deal of group and non-group affairs are transacted because of their fear of "acting out." For some therapists, the therapeutic experience is so special that it has to be separated from being contaminated by the rest of life.

I don't consider therapy and life as two separate categories. From my point of view, therapy is an extension of life. I am particularly grateful that the members of the group see one another in more ordinary social circumstances and even that they have a chance to see one another with less intensity and perhaps less distortion. One of the dangers of this fraternization, however, is the possibility that the members will band together and attack

me and decide for their own purposes what I am thinking and
how wrong it is. This is more likely when just two or at most
three persons form an alliance to support one another's resistances. Although this situation can be difficult to cope with, I
still prefer group members to have the opportunity of meeting to
form friendships, even if the foundation of the friendship turns
out to be based on a mutual need to protect themselves from me.
Thereby the group may provide not only therapy but friendship,
occasionally perhaps even love and sometimes a chance to unite
against therapy itself. This is a pretty potent range of possibilities and one that is not available to anyone in individual
sessions.

Still another important aspect of the group is the opportunity
for members to learn a great deal about the intimate lives of
others. All too often a person's intimate relationships are limited
to just the members of his family and, if he is lucky, one or two
friends. Indeed, for too many persons who come to see me there
are virtually *no* intimate relationships, either friend *or* family.
Individual therapy provides a means where I can serve as a
special kind of an intimate, a friend, though one always somewhat
suspect because of my role. In the group no one has to be
intimate, and these gifts when made may be freely given, or, if
not present, the group provides an opportunity to find out under
what terms intimacy or friendship is possible.

Regardless of whether or not you are looking for intimacy in a
group, it cannot be avoided. You may not be willing to take part
in its expression, but you cannot isolate yourself from being a
spectator when others are honestly sharing their tenderest feelings, their most vulnerable wounds.

For some group members, this opportunity to learn about the
private lives of others, to identify with these lives, to share
intimacy, to form friendships, makes participation in the group
an exceedingly powerful experience, an exceedingly moving
event. That is, for many members the group is the first time they
begin to know and/or experience anything about possibilities in

human relationships. All too often at the start of therapy a person has no significant relationships. The group then is particularly important as a place to experiment with other people in a protected atmosphere.

There is another way in which group therapy differs from individual therapy, one that has been hinted at earlier. Group therapy offers a sense of drama that is heightened as a person struggles with his demons. Perhaps *theater* is a better word. I have already commented on the presence of the audience. At times the audience spontaneously offers suggestions, interpretations, tears or even catcalls. Sometimes I improvise a psychodrama for members to participate in; sometimes I structure an event so that everyone is involved; sometimes they all spontaneously begin to argue or become embroiled. We do not know what will happen next, how psychodramas will be enacted, what eruptions will occur, what the denouement will be. Within the minimal structure I provide by focusing on an individual or setting up an experiment for him to perform there is an atmosphere of tension and excitement. Occasionally, when something doesn't work out, frustration and boredom develop; but that, too, becomes a part of what there is at hand to work with. This sense of theater is not present to the same degree in individual sessions, although some of the individual sessions can be very thrilling. Yet our cast of two limits possibilities. Instead, individual therapy provides that delicious feeling of pure selfishness: This time is all mine; I can use it as I please. This person is here to sit and listen to my problems and to no one else's. No one in group therapy can get away with that attitude for long.

My own work is certainly different in individual therapy and in group therapy. When I first acted as a group leader I was tense as well as excited by the sessions; and when I begin a new group, I still feel this way. I need to connect not only with the person on whom I am focusing but with the other members as well. Some group leaders feel content to sit back and let whatever happens happen, but within limits I want to be more active, to try and ensure, if I can, that the group is a rewarding event. Fritz Perls' way of running a group was to permit the other members to observe his work with one person. I prefer a good deal of group interaction, and when a group is going well, when the members have a good grasp of themselves and other persons, I withdraw and let them handle the situation themselves. Many therapists feel so threatened by groups that they do not offer this option to those whom they see. If a therapist is concerned about power and control, then a group is a threat because it takes so much effort to control twelve people instead of just one. Some therapists feel they need to be in charge of everything that is happening, and only in a "dead" group is this so.

One of the kinds of things that can happen is that one member will become active and in effect elect himself to be my co-thera-pist in running the group. For many, the role of therapist is attractive and appealing. Often the power of the therapist is coveted. I am content to let whoever wants to usurp me or join me do so as part of his own growth. Depending on who this person is and how well he handles his self-awarded authority, the group will take various steps. Often at least one or two members will become jealous and competitive: How dare he assume this role which I myself would like to play? How dare he arrogate to himself some of the sacred power of the leader? If a person is wildly off base in trying to play co-therapist, then the group will quickly cut him down to size, either by ignoring his comments or more directly letting him know that they do not find his authori-tative comments very satisfying. When a person is really good at acting as co-therapist, it usually is a sign that he has at least grasped many of the techniques of therapy. More importantly for him, I want to know if he can integrate this ability in his own life instead of just using it to imitate me.

One final difference between group and individual sessions is that in an individual session you may assign me a similarity to important people in your life—father, mother, brother, boss, co-worker, enemy. The range is limited by our limitation; there are just the two of us. The range is also limited because it is difficult to imagine me as your younger sister, girlfriend, grandfather. There are a greater number of personalities to respond to in the group, a greater range of roles to experiment with, more individuals to respond to in a genuine way that is not inhibited by the therapeutic encounter. Too often the therapist is treated as the fountain of knowledge and given exaggerated respect so that the encounters in sessions are too polite. With group members the person experiences more equality and feels freer to respond directly without the fear of reprisal from an irate therapist. With all the possibilities in group to share intimately and directly in one another's lives, group members often enter into a relationship that approaches the feeling of family. As time passes and they begin to share a common past, and as they partake fully in honest exchanges, it is not uncommon for genuine outside friendships to develop and for group members to feel closer to one another than to their own families. Unfortunately, for too many people family life is so bounded by evasions, hidden tensions, jealousy, withdrawal, dishonesty, hostility and fear that what little genuine love there is becomes shriveled or lost. The family feeling developed in group can be vital and nourishing. Occasions such as a member's departure for another part of the country or because of the ending of therapy can be very moving experiences. The entrance of a new member to the group can also result in a wide range of dislocated feelings for all parties, both new and old members. Tightly knit families do not easily admit new in-laws. Established neighborhoods often test new neighbors before becoming friendly, and this also can happen in the group.

While individual therapy can be a deeply moving experience when two people honestly confront each other, when the range is successfully widened to include a dozen persons with vastly different backgrounds and experiences and when it works emotionally, then the group therapeutic experience is even more dramatic and exciting, more electric and brilliant.

9 . Another Group Meeting

I want to include the report of another group session to indicate how valuable group therapy can be.

Sol told me in his private session that he wanted to work in the group. He has had a difficult time with the group. When he first entered it he was just recovering from a long, painful divorce and eagerly sought the chance to meet new people, to get support and, as he said, feedback. In fact, one of his demands when he began private therapy was that I have a group available so that he could participate.

At first he had a passionate attachment to the group, finding it just what he had hoped for, perhaps because he was determined to find what he was searching for and therefore did not look at the group realistically. His sexual experiences had been severely limited before coming to therapy, and he was very embarrassed by and ashamed of his own sexual organs and his limited sexual experience. One night he asked the group point-blank if anyone objected to his undressing, and before taking a poll he quickly stripped and paraded around the room. The response by other members of the group was varied. Some, like me, had no particular objection but little interest. Some of the women were upset, particularly those who themselves had problems of sexual intimacy. A few wept in shame and fear. Conversely, one man hugged Sol and told him how much he had admired him for his bravery.

Sol was confused by the response of the group. In his own mind he had anticipated approval for what he considered his openness, and he felt betrayed when it was not forthcoming.

On another occasion the same man who had hugged him so warmly blasted him mercilessly for what he felt was Sol's dishonest attempt to win favor among group members and to strangle his own anger. Once again Sol was full of anguish at what had happened in the group, and he withdrew from participation. Another issue complicated his response to the group. As he gained some sexual confidence he approached one of the members, Fanny, who was mourning the loss of a lover whom she had almost married. Although she was flattered by Sol's attention, she was not interested in becoming Sol's mate.

So it happened that Sol, who had wanted intensely to join a group, now found himself angry with the members, hurt and withdrawn. He felt that he had to be very careful with the group members. I had watched all of this develop with little participation on my own part. Sol would have to look out for himself. I was not prepared to take on the role of his protector. I thought it was important for him to learn how he first saw the group in an unreal, idealized fashion and how at the same time he made demands that others were not prepared to accept, so that he could later feel justified in his anger and then withdraw by blaming the group.

That morning in his private session we had worked on his relation with Gloria, a girl he also idealized and believed he had had a perfect relationship with for the first three months. During the subsequent six months he had been quarreling with her. Sol had finally decided not to see Gloria on any terms whatsoever. He was very angry with her because at their last meeting she had been particularly loving and friendly but had refused to end the evening by sleeping with him.

My idea of a good group session is one where the group members are largely responsible for what happens. I am there as a catalyst. I try especially hard not to have preconceptions about what is going to happen or about what should happen. I try to limit myself to a hypothesis about what might happen, but even here I try to be free to accept what doesn't happen as equally exciting, useful or fruitful.

Last night was the night before Thanksgiving, the beginning of the holiday period. Macy's, Gimbels and Saks may pray all year for this season when peace on earth, good will toward man help ring up the cash registers, but therapists know that this is the winter of discontent, the time when people bitterly relive all the miseries of their childhood, when thoughts of suicide are rife and when good folk who feel they can no longer survive take themselves to therapists. Here is how the Thanksgiving season began in the group just last night.

In the pre-group arrival, as I prepare the coffee, Heather informs me with a tense laugh that she wants to scream because one hour before she was to leave for group her baby-sitter canceled. She then spent the remaining hour desperately trying to locate a baby-sitter, and then Liz, another member of the group, arranged for a baby-sitter. I invite Heather to scream. She wants to let off tension, and she herself has proposed this method. Why not? I have no neighbors to complain. Perhaps it is not *bien élévé* to scream, since Heather has been raised in Europe as a proper young woman. But no, her family is quite bohemian, writers, painters, sculptors. We are well beyond that *politesse*. Or at least some of us are, as we shall see. Is Heather unwilling to deal with an intellectual understanding of her problems? Well, I am responding to her legitimate rage, from my point of view. So I say, "Why not scream, Heather?" She does so with great glee. It is a pretty good scream, loud, long, piercing. She laughs, but I feel she is still unfinished. Some of her tension is released in the scream, some of her rage is vented, some of her frustration has been expressed, but not all. I invite Heather to continue with another scream if she wants to. She does so. This time the scream is deeper, shorter, truncated. She has had enough. Is all of Heather's rage dealt with? No, I will not take on at this moment the responsibility for dealing with all of her rage, with her unhappiness as an American child in Europe, as a student at Sarah Lawrence, trying to sculpt and being seduced by her father and her father's friends, as an unhappy wife who at this very moment is about to separate from her husband and live alone with her two children. No, I am only trying at this moment to find a means so that Heather can feel reasonably comfortable to stay with the group session that is about to begin. My goals are limited: If I take care of this minute, then it will be easier to take care of the next.

Moe is a businessman, more conventional in his point of view. If I asked him to scream he would not oblige me. From his point of view screaming is poor form, bad behavior, undignified, something to shun and avoid. Moe's parents, immigrants from Europe, screamed and screamed at each other while he was growing up, and he hated it. He wants to be a refined, cultured man of the middle class, not like his vulgar parents. Of course, he gets in angry bouts with his wife; of course, he gets drunk, insults people viciously, but from his point of view he doesn't raise his voice, and he expiates his guilt by feeling remorse. He tolerates this kind of behavior in other group members he is not especially close to, but he still cannot understand why intelligent ladies and gentlemen will willingly choose to scream. He says somewhat sarcastically to Heather, to me, to the group each time that Heather screams, "Did it do any good? Did it help?" No one answers him. I choose not to answer either. Let him decide for himself. A difficult task, for Moe finds he doubts himself on all decisions. He knows right from wrong in terms of limited conventional wisdom, but he is paralyzed to make his own mind up, to act. (Eight months will pass before Moe is willing to explore and express his own anger in the group. After this happens he is all smiles and grasps my hand warmly.)

Mary has approached me in the kitchen. She started a new job in September at a black nursery in Harlem as the only white teacher. She is the head teacher, with two assistants, a black

female and a Puerto Rican male. She has been having trouble
with her assistant, May, with the principal and with two of the
children, Shirley and Leo. She says that she would like to work
that evening because she thinks that the trouble she is having
now is reminiscent of her difficulty at a progressive school, where
she was fired four years ago because she could not control a fifth-
grade class. At that time she had been a patient in psychoanalysis
for a number of years and talked endlessly with her therapist
about her difficulty with the children. When she first came to see
me she was working as a typist for a physicist. Gradually she
returned to teaching, taking additional course work in nursery
education, and after several brief, stormy teaching assignments
she was until just recently relatively happy about the children
and the school in Harlem.

Mary begins a narrative about her difficulties in handling
Shirley and Leo, particularly during rest periods. Shirley and Leo
are quite compliant with Juan, her Puerto Rican assistant, but
refuse to lie down when Mary is in charge.

I interrupt Mary and ask her to be Shirley for us right now.
My guess is that Mary is responding to something in Shirley that
is also very powerfully unfinished in Mary, and rather than try to
see if I can elicit this from her by a lengthy series of questions, I
want Mary to explore for herself in a more direct fashion who
Shirley is for her. Mary's face fills with naughty glee, a wicked
smile, provocative laughing eyes. Mary kicks and pushes furni-
ture around, shuffles and says in a mocking, childish voice, "Yes,
dear; yes, dear; yes, dear," and then turns to us. "She always says
that. 'Yes, dear!' "

Mary sits down. It is clear to her and everyone else that she has
enjoyed playing Shirley, being naughty, disobeying. I ask Mary
in which way Shirley and Mary's male cat Vanilla are alike and
different. I have invented a riddle, a toy for Mary to play with.
She makes a face at me. She begins skeptically, "Well, one is a
girl and the other is a cat." She laughs and continues with some
annoyance. "You mean that it's O.K. for Vanilla to be naughty—

I don't mind—but I do when Shirley is." Yes, Mary has found the answer to my riddle, so now I ask her what the difference is between them, why she will accept Vanilla's misbehavior but not Shirley's. Mary makes another face. She knots her fingers into a fist. "Because Shirley and Leo have no guilt. They do what they want, and they have no guilt!" And in what way is Mary different from Shirley and Leo? Mary answers with a face filled with hatred, leering at me. She raises her hand in anger. "Because I am filled with guilt when I do what I'm not supposed to." I then finish the paradigm for her. "So you're going to teach them how to be guilty, to make them suffer, just as you do, to know right from wrong." "Yes," she hisses at me, again her face contorted by anger. "You bet!" Mary continues, excited now at the opportunity of telling us how terrible she is. "I want to smack her, I want to hurt her. When I grab her arm, I twist it and I'm glad. I want to punish her, and I enjoy it. Yes"—she leers at me—"I enjoy these sado-masochistic games, or whatever else you want to call them, yes, I do!"

Mary raises her hand, as if to strike Shirley, and I ask her to become her hand, about to lash out. She quickly obliges and pours out more rage. Mary complains bitterly with a look of contempt on her face. "Shirley and Leo know that I'm just a milquetoast, that they can get away with anything, that I will let them get away with it. Well, I won't. They're going to pay."

At this point I also want Mary to be aware, lest she become overwhelmed with guilt at her own hatred, that she has other resources, other feelings for Shirley. I ask her to turn now to her other hand, the hand that has been ready to restrain the hand that was ready to deal the blow. Mary then calms herself by reciting all of the reasons why she doesn't want to strike Shirley. Her voice has changed. When she spoke as the hostile hand her voice was tough, harsh, brutal. Now as the restraining hand she is sensible, sensitive, gentle. She can hear the difference in her voice; she can appreciate better what she is responding to in

Shirley and Leo, what is still unsolved in herself, what interferes with her ability to handle disobedient children. We pause because the incident is finished, but we have not finished working with Mary.

Heather addresses Mary about the recent past. Heather has invited Mary to spend either Thanksgiving or Christmas with her and her children. Mary has refused, saying that she can't do that; she has to go home to be with her father and mother in Connecticut. Heather becomes more current. "Tonight, when you were talking about Shirley, I was reminded so keenly of when I visited your parents' home and how they behave like milquetoasts, and so do you when you are with them. I don't recognize you. You never stand up to them. You're so afraid to say 'no' to them."

Mary fights back. She is angry with Heather. Mary says, "You don't understand. You just think you do." She screws her face up maliciously, defiantly. "I *want* to go home for Thanksgiving."

Heather asks, "Then what about Christmas?"

"And Christmas too!"

Heather will not be put off. "I think that you're too guilty to do what you want to on the holidays, that you believe you have to be a good little girl and go home to Mommy and Daddy."

Mary is enraged. "I'll do what I want to. I'll be who I want to. That's enough for me, and it had better be enough for everyone else."

I intervene and ask Mary what she would like to do if she doesn't go home to her parents.

She continues angrily, "Then I just want to sit at home alone, masturbate and stuff myself. I'll eat and eat by myself. I want to be alone and not see anyone." She is almost crying as she says this, but she is also quite angry and defiant.

I decide to try and raise the stakes higher and ask Mary to have a fantasy about the future. "Suppose," I say, "it is ten years from now. Can you tell us about your Thanksgiving?"

Mary shakes her head yes defiantly. "Yes. I am a fat, middle-aged old maid"— she is still crying—"and I go home for Thanksgiving to stay with my parents."

Her face is red with anger. I raise the stakes higher. "Suppose that your father is dead."

Mary will not be deterred. "Then I should go home and live with my mother."

I try to make the fantasy less palatable. "Yes, you might be principal of the school in the local town and you could live at home."

"That's right!" Mary is half crying, half choking with rage, but she will not let go.

I decide there is little purpose to be served in continuing along this line. Mary is determined to torture herself, us; she is prepared to hang on to her guilt and self-hatred, her spite and stubbornness unless we can help her find a way out.

I suggest that she vent her rage by pounding a pillow. I don't often suggest such a mechanical means of dealing with fury, but Mary, I believe, will not be available to words or logic at this point. She complies and we all go through an excruciating agony while Mary pounds the pillow with varying degrees of rage, anguish and moaning and groaning sounds, some from deep within her, some from her throat. Mary is urged by the group to keep trying to express some of her bottled-up rage, and as she pounds furiously she feels some easing of her loathing. Once she stops, however, she quickly recovers and verbally begins to lunge at herself once again, pounding her fist into her leg at the same time. When Mary gets stuck in this rage of self-loathing, she will not easily take comfort. The group sit morosely as one attempt after another fails to help Mary let go. Finally, in desperation, Henry asks if there is anything that Mary will accept from the group. Is there any way she will consent to let us do anything for her at all? She says with a bitter, ironic laugh that she would like a cracker. I quickly get up and fetch her a cracker box from the kitchen. She eats one or two slowly and then extends her hand to me. I shake my head no and instead invite her to sit on my lap. She refuses, but then without too much prodding she sits on my lap and we hold hands. Fairly quickly she begins to sob in the most violent way, her whole body shaking. She reaches out to Heather, and we both hold her as she adds wailing to her sobs. Mary's crying continues for more than five minutes at the same explosive level. She has left my lap, and Heather comforts her like a child. Later Mary feels greatly relieved.

A long time ago Mary became stuck in a pattern of feeling guilty, attempting to compensate by feeling very special and wonderful, loathing herself for fantasies of being superior, not delivering, and somehow hoping someone else would free her from her tortures. This evening we have not solved Mary's problems. She has had them for a long time. What I hope is that we have made it possible for her to step outside them in an important way and to see them clearly, if only for an evening. She has been able to accept help; she has been just as nasty as she could be without being made to feel guilty or having to pay a price. If something more comes out of this evening for Mary, then fine; but if not, then we will try again another evening.

As we work, from week to week, from minute to minute, Mary continues the same patterns but less intensely, with less involvement, and gradually she begins to add new kinds of ways of living. But all of this takes time.

Now Sol reminds me that he would like to work. The atmosphere in the group is still tense because of all of the emotion Mary aroused. Sol begins to tell us of his anger with his ex-girlfriend, Gloria, who no longer wants to sleep with him. As he begins to talk, the women in the group very quickly become offended. Sol is not aware of how belittling he is toward Gloria and how his own need to be reassured of his sexual prowess makes him look a male chauvinist. Sol feels attacked by the women, as indeed he is, and is surprised. What has he done wrong? he asks, and the women try to explain that he is more concerned about whether or not Gloria will fuck than what is happening between them. Sol becomes irate, and the women attack him like harpies. All unaware, he has asked for it, and now he has gotten it. Sol is completely taken aback, so I step in and try to explain to him what has happened, what part he has played in unleashing this storm of hatred from the women, particularly as he seems to feel so innocent. He feels hurt and betrayed by the group, including me.

Jean is particularly enraged. She lashes out at Sol and tells him how disgusted she is and how much she hates him. Jean's hatred is expressed with flashing eyes, a twisted mouth and her head thrust forward. Sol wants to run for cover and does so in the only way he is comfortable; he withdraws and becomes superior. He becomes contemptuous and at the same time outraged and hurt. Jean, like a terrier, will not let go. Sol can no longer hear her or respond clearly to what is happening. I try to use some of my therapeutic capital and spend it on cooling Sol down, trying to see how much he can take in of what is happening. He is confused but willing to admit that although he doesn't understand what has happened, he recognizes it must have something to do with him; that although he does not feel guilty he has to learn how he provoked all of this.

Jean has calmed down sufficiently so that she tries to let Sol in on what is happening on her part. First, she is angry with her own boyfriend because of a similar kind of chauvinist point of view. But worse, she feels intimidated by her boyfriend's demands and often complies, even though she is furious with him for asking and for her own submission. More directly, she also sees in Sol a hated reflection of her own behavior. Just as Sol came to the group, hoping for support against Gloria, wanting the group to sanction his behavior, so Jean recognizes her own wish for the group to take care of her, to tell her what to do, and if not the group, why, then, a strong man. Jean feels she tries to squelch these feelings, and here is Sol blatantly indulging himself. It is more than Jean can bear. Sol is still shaken. He knows something more about himself and how he affects others. He is not finished, but we stop working with him at this moment. He has more than enough to chew over.

Besides, Henry wants some time. He is furious with Heather, his wife, because she has asked him to leave the house. He lashes out vituperatively against her for forcing him out of the house during the holiday season. Heather tries to correct him, stating that he is welcome to stay through Thanksgiving or, if he leaves now, then he is still welcome at Thanksgiving with her and the children. He has little interest in hearing this.

The members of the group know Henry well enough to know that when he is so angry it is likely that below his anger are other emotions, especially fear. We ask him to tell us about his fear. He drops his anger and then tells of his fear of being left alone, of being unloved, of not having a home or a family. He tells of his jealousy of Mary and her closeness with Heather. Henry is eloquent and powerful when he is expressing his strong emotions. We have all been deeply moved by Mary's pain and then later Jean's anger and Sol's hurt. Now we feel almost torn apart by Henry's range of emotions about separating from Heather.

Suddenly Joel explodes. He screams, "I can't stand it any more. I just can't take it. All these emotions. These feelings are just too much for me."

For most of his adult life Joel has tried to pretend he doesn't have feelings. He justified this position by aping the strong, silent screen heroes of the 1930s movies, and although many of the members of the group protest, they recognize that there are all too many American men who try to avoid their strong feelings if they cannot be stated in a flat, controlled way. Joel has gradually been experimenting with letting go of this tough-guy façade, and now tonight he tries to stay with his feelings. The evening has been wearing for all of us, but he particularly finds it intolerable. Henry and other members of the group try to comfort him by holding him and stroking him. Henry himself is much calmer now that he is aware of how strong his jealous feelings are and how frightened he is of being alone. Joel gradually subsides in his outpourings and feels somewhat guilty but he also shouts that grown men don't behave like this. But there is a gleam in his eyes, because he has dared not to behave like a grown man, even though John Wayne would disapprove.

10 . On Being a Group Member

How can the group help in a particular instance? Melissa was
terrified of anger—her own, her husband's, her children's. When
I first asked her to be angry, she froze. No sounds would come
from her throat; her usually pallid face became ashen. At that
time, all that was necessary was for Melissa to experience how
petrified she was of expressing anger, even in a controlled situation, in a playful manner.

Later she experienced her husband's anger (he was a member
of the group) and with the support of the group was able to
withstand it without collapsing: sobbing, giving in to his rage,
blaming herself. Still later she began to express her own anger,
sometimes as a blinding rage, sometimes as a choked fury. Here
too the group played a part in letting Melissa know that if she
vented her rage and fury, this did not make her a horrible
person, never to be forgiven, nor would she annihilate others by
her anger. Finally, Melissa had an opportunity in the group to
become at peace with her anger, to accept her feelings, to recognize their value in indicating where she stood, to help vitalize
her life, to liberate her subservience to her husband's greater
wrath, to be both loving and angry with her children, whichever
made sense in a particular situation.

Melissa's husband, Enrico, was suspicious and threatened by
others. At first he tried to be useful to the group by assuming a
position of strength, offering whatever was demanded as a basis

for a relationship. When he realized he could not sustain the burden of all his proffered aid, he withdrew from the group. Here he was able to sense his isolation and his pseudo contact. Now began a stormy period of group membership that he found extremely oppressive. It was hard for him to attend sessions, to sit through them; sometimes he sat in a corner away from the others. During this period Enrico's own needs began to emerge. Instead of offering great strengths, he demanded great indulgence. He tried to provoke me and the other group members. He insulted us with interpretations that were probably his own projections; he bellowed his rage so fully that when he really got going all the women in the group were in tears. He found that he could express his own insecurity and anger with few consequences. He began to learn how potent his anger was, that he could intimidate others with it. He discovered that he often blew up not when he was angry but when he was frightened, that he was ashamed of his fear. Later, when he became angry, instead of blowing up, he was encouraged to explore whether or not he was frightened. On other occasions he was asked to blow up deliberately.

He became the resident expert in anger, and, like a maestro, he was asked to see if he could develop a wide range of anger from fortissimo to the barest audible tremolo. On other occasions, members of the group and I answered his anger directly so that he experienced our anger, discovered what it was like to be on the receiving end. Throughout all of this period he was accepted as a full member of the group. Over time, Enrico learned to control his anger, to use it sparingly and with purpose, to recognize his own fears and the part anger played in isolating him from others. Then Enrico's earlier strengths began to emerge once again. His contributions to others were less strained and distorted. He became good friends with other members and could give and take aid. All of this took nearly three years of participation in the group, but it is questionable whether it could have happened at all without the group.

Michael was deeply ashamed of his homosexuality. From his point of view all straight people would have to shun him. He could make no exceptions. He had no awareness that it was his own condemnation of homosexuals that was plaguing him. In the group he found acceptance of his homosexuality, but he continued to deny the validity of the experience. He thought the other members of the group were only pretending to accept him. With time, however, his experiences with group members transcended their verbal acceptance. When Olivia was grief-stricken by the death of her brother, she chose Michael to mourn with. When Alfred, the group jock, spoke about his own homosexual feelings that he had never dared to express directly, he sobbed and hugged Michael. When Harriet separated from her husband, she asked Michael to comfort her. When Michael spoke of his own continued loneliness and misery in looking for homosexual partners, members of the group offered genuine sympathy and identified their own loneliness as similar. Gradually, over time, Michael began to feel less of a pariah, returned to visit his parents in the South, found a place in a family that he had felt was forever closed to him, became more open in his relations with heterosexuals, even recognized that he was using his own homosexuality as a means of demanding special treatment, of justifying his withdrawal from social relations.

I would like to emphasize that in each instance there were no necessary major breakthroughs, even at our most dramatic moments, even when there was a highly charged, highly excited group. After the excitement had subsided, either that night or the next day or the next week, there remained the difficult task of integrating what had occurred, of finding a means of assimilating the new awareness into an ongoing way of functioning. Often (and this is difficult for an impatient therapist like myself, eager to be successful) the gains of a group session are "lost," receded into the background, only to be rediscovered three, six months later. Sometimes, alas, new skills are put away, not to emerge at all after an initial period of trial and success. Sometimes the new skills are used in life but carefully shielded from the therapist, so that they must be inferred. After all, why please him? The person forms his own destiny, lives his own life in his own way. His purpose in therapy, group or otherwise, is to make his own path in his own life, not to please a therapist's concept of "mental health."

Timothy had spent more than fifteen years in psychoanalysis and was still a drug addict. I insisted from the beginning that I would not set a goal with him that he would be drug-free as a result of his treatment. I sensed an attempt on his part to start gathering weapons to use to thwart me. From his first session he tried to tell me what an awful person he was, to build a case against himself. When I asked him what he could tell me that was good about himself he almost wept. Wasn't this how you interested therapists, by confessing how terrible you were and then keeping their interest by proving that you were even worse than they had suspected?

Clearly I had to be prepared for elaborate tricks, ploys, machinations, and I was not disappointed. Timothy delighted in finding new plots to weave, in proving how hopeless he was and then, when he felt more comfortable with me, how crazy I was for thinking I could be accepted by him. On occasion he was particularly friendly and confessed how much better he felt and that maybe he had a chance for a better life. I told him that I had long ago learned from one of my eminent professors at Harvard that after an offer of friendliness I would do well to look forward to a stab in the back. So that when Timothy offered his, I would be prepared and not make him pay for it. The stabs came, time and time again, until he gradually came to recognize their occurrence too. He said that if he permitted himself to feel close and open, then he had to protect himself by inciting hostility.

Timothy was fairly eager to join a group. He had been a member of a group made up of drug addicts for two years. He had been forced out because he would not stay off drugs and would not obey the system that had been worked out for that type of therapy. I anticipated that he would not be an easy group member but felt I needed the additional support of other people to make an important impact on him.

At the beginning of his participation in the group Timothy tried to lead the members toward accepting a whole series of rules. Largely these rules were taken from the type of therapy he had previously been a part of and which presumably he had rejected, just as they had rejected him. He particularly tried to impose all kinds of "courtesy" rules. Members *should not* whisper to one another when another member was working. The group *should* start promptly at 7:30 P.M. and members *should not* be permitted to come late. Each person *should* have a turn in order. Most of the group members just laughed, but he persisted in a kind of outraged justice, and still the others refused to take the gambit. Timothy then bellowed at the others for their lack of serious purpose and then at me. A frequent complaint was "What kind of a group are you running?" We all refused to become as rigid as he wanted, and he felt sure that he had a group of liberal nuts whom he would have little trouble in manipulating. We tried in every way we knew to get him to accept us, and he tried in every way he knew to put us off. We asked him to be Steve McQueen, and he loved it. We asked him to play Cotton Mather and he gloried in it. We asked him to play Chicken Little, "a gutless wonder," two of his catch phrases, and he sniveled. On his part, he told us horror stories to put people off: how he beat his wife, how he threw his daughter out of the house, how he ignored his mother, how racially prejudiced he was. The members of the group told him point-blank that they could not take him seriously, that from their point of view he represented a parody of right-wing smugness.

Timothy had other ways of keeping us away. If he did work, then he had a routine. First he would present a problem that he said was difficult and almost insoluble for him. Then as the group worked with him he had a major breakthrough and he became terribly serious. "You mean that that's all there is to it?"

And then the total acceptance. Except nobody believed him. But he was safe until the next time he worked.

He studied us all, me in particular, taking notes, trying to detect dishonesty, inconsistencies, stupidity. And then he pounced, trying to shock and terrorize. It didn't work, not one bit. Then he began to have tantrums. He threatened to break a chair over my head, to sock another man, to strangle a woman. We called his bluffs. So he started walking out, and we let him, but he came back within a few minutes. As he put it himself, when he got outside he figured, Where am I going to go from here? This is pretty good stuff, so I better go back.

Despite all of the carrying on in the group, Timothy began to have a better relationship with his wife and a more open relationship with his daughter, who had moved back into the house. Then he started to skip sessions for fairly good reasons, and at first I consented. Then the reasons became more obviously phony. I pointed out that I wanted him to make his own decision, either to stay with the group and attend regularly or to stop coming altogether. I told him I did not want him to drop in. He was furious. He called me a Hitler, claimed that now I had revealed my true colors, showed myself for the totalitarian he always knew I was. And when the shouting had died down, he elected to continue working in the group, and after he had made his own decision, only then would he demote me from being a Hitler.

Gradually Timothy began to trust the group more. He spoke of his fears of being crazy, and when the group didn't believe this either and asked him to be crazy with us, he obliged and had a wonderful time shouting and stamping his feet. So did the rest of us. He also complained about all of his crazy feelings running through him, and when we guessed that these might be excitement that he kept blocking, he permitted himself to flow with these feelings and performed a terrific kinetic dance that thrilled him and us as well. He said at other times that he really couldn't work in the group, that he was too weak. We took him at his word, and he rested prone on a couch while all the group members took turns waiting on him and making him comfortable.

Timothy was Jewish and felt he could not trust any Gentiles not to hate his "Jew-face," but surprisingly he found himself making friends with people in the group who weren't Jewish. He said in mock seriousness, How can Gentiles who were serious about themselves choose as therapist me, another Jew-face, and how did I have the courage to accept them? Didn't I know that sooner or later they would turn on me? When some of the pretty women in the group, both Jewish and Gentile, would embrace Timothy, although he genuinely enjoyed the experience he tried to pass it all off as just nothing, but he was impressed. All of these sessions made their inroads. Some theorists hold out for a position that indicates that particular sessions or the handling of a special issue are crucial in therapy. With Timothy, we had to prove ourselves over and over again, and even then, once he had accepted us, he could slip back, granted the circumstances.

Timothy is no longer afraid of being sent to a concentration camp. He feels more secure about his abilities as a businessman, his relationships with his family are more solid, and he has made a good friend. He still takes drugs, but he claims that this too will pass. If so, I and the group will be there, doing our part. And if not, then his life is still richer and fuller than when he came three years ago.

11 . Ending

How do we end?

We have been seeing each other for a number of years, once a week privately, once a week in group. During this time I have come to know you very well. Yet I have had to change my view as you changed as a result of our work together. (There, I can use the word *work* now, and I know you will understand it.)

I have watched you become less shy, stronger, more solid, sure of yourself, able to complete unfinished business from the past or able to make yourself comfortable enough so that you can live easily with what is still unfinished.

You still have sore spots—a tendency to try to control more than you are able to, a belief that you can continue to rely on charm and good looks to get you through a difficult situation, a truce with your father instead of peace.

You have watched me change. I too have my unfinished business to attend to. You see that I am both more patient and less patient, more casual about drugs and less tolerant about cigarettes. The remnants of my professional manner are nearly all vanished. You have never seen me in a white shirt, a tie or a suit; you have never heard me address anyone as Miss, Ms. or Mr.

Now you wonder, Is it time to stop? *Stop* is a better word than *end*, just as *stop* is a better word than *finish*. We never end, we never finish; we stop. Growth and development continue throughout life; all we decide is at this moment we will cease our joint explorations. But, you protest, there is more. How do I know that I'm done, that I'm finished?

There you betray yourself. We are never finished, except when we die. That's the end, the finish. We can stop our meetings, but each of us goes on, unendingly.

I know, you want a diploma, a certificate of good mental health, a talisman to use in the future when bad times come, and they will. I can give you my blessing for what it is worth. But that is not a certificate of health.

Instead, let me ask you to write your own certificate of health. Tell me all the ways in which you feel good about yourself. Let me see how you look at yourself right now.

And now tell me all the issues that are still unfinished in your life. Now look at the two lists. How do you feel about each one? You see there is more. Now do you still want to stop? Yes, you feel you have had as much as you want at this time. Of course there is more, but you want to go at it on your own for a while, to see what that is like.

Fine. Then we are free to make our arrangements as to what happens next. Shall we meet every other week for the next month or two, or shall we meet only four more times and then stop? We can decide between us.

No. Your sense of what remains unfinished is too huge. You were tired of coming. It all seems so endless. You wanted to test me, to trick me, and now you realize you do want to keep coming. Are you sure? Are you just feeling frightened now that you want to go off on your own? No, no. I push anyway. What if I decided that you were finished and that we had to stop? Would it be easier to leave if I accept the burden of your stopping?

You see, sometimes I find that I am being tested, and I find the situation unpleasant. Ideally you come here because of a desire to do something with your life. But once here that desire can fade, and instead you feel it is much more important to play games with me. One of these games is to say, I don't think I want to keep coming to see you any longer. Now convince me that I should. I don't like to convince anyone to do anything. That is part of being an adult—to make up your own mind. And yet, if I say nothing, then you may leave, partly in spite, partly feeling I don't care, partly taking my silence as agreement.

So reluctantly I may tell you my view of what remains and what you may be trying to avoid. I point out as best I can that my view is only my view, but you insist on making it into something more. That already is a sign that something needs attending to. You feel relieved. You only wanted to bait me, to prove you could leave if you wanted to. You wanted to let me know that I don't control you. And so we go on.

When you are not playing games, when you feel you want to stop, that you have gotten as much as you can, that you have confidence in the future, then we can stop.

We can stop. But you go on. The aim of our work together is for you to learn how to be your own therapist, how to heal yourself. Once we stop, your life continues with its stress, conflicts, threats, as well as its pleasures, joys, excitement. As you meet these new adventures, you can experience them as a whole person. And where you meet blocks, resistance, anxiety, misery, then you can still carry forward and get through by yourself.

This does not mean I am forgotten. You may have imaginary conversations with me, dialogues; you may have taken parts of me that are still not wholly you, and so you may hear my voice within you speaking. You may, if you are particularly upset, call me for a consultation. I will not have forgotten you, and I am agreeable to see you when a particular crisis of huge dimension arises. I repeat, we have stopped, but we have not ended.

I have my own feelings to deal with when you talk of stopping. During the time we worked together, I have come to be genuinely fond of you, even to love you. As we struggled together we shared a profound experience. I felt your love (and hate), and now I feel your loss in my own life. I will miss our sessions, fighting alongside you, against you, working through what is troubling you, both of us deeply engaged in finding out what is hidden, how to free your energy. This is my work, and for me too our work stops. But I also am not finished. I have my own feelings, memories, thoughts of what has happened to both of us. You have been an important part of my life too.

Perhaps your decision is unclear. You want to stay and you want to leave. If you are importantly unfinished with your therapy, you may find that the only means by which you can leave is to get angry. I find this painful, but it is part of what exists for you at this moment. You have had as much therapy as you want, but you also feel guilty about stopping. You do not want to face me, your feelings of guilt or your feelings of loss. So instead you make up some reason to be angry, something to justify your leaving. If you are genuinely angry, if I have been stupid, then we can talk about this. Indeed, this is part of what therapy is. But no, you are angry and cannot, will not, talk about it. You must leave with your righteousness and your anger intact. I cannot make you stay. I do not want to, but I ask you to think it over and let me know if you have any second thoughts. Meanwhile, I request that we at least talk about it one more time, next week. This delaying tactic may permit you to cool some of your anger, but if you really mean to use it as a means to leave, then you will probably telephone me and cancel the next session or send me a letter explaining that no purpose would be served by our meeting once more. If you are this determined, perhaps you are right. Later, once safely out of therapy, you may have other thoughts and feelings. We will see.

Our revels now are ended. You prepare to depart. Shall you cry? Your eyes mist. Shall we embrace? I would like to. Have you my blessing? For what it is worth, you have it. I would rather you have your own. I think of T. S. Eliot's line in *The Cocktail Party:* "Go and work out your salvation with diligence." Although Eliot's phrasing is quasi-religious, I prefer to interpret it in a spiritual way. Take, then, my benediction.

We no longer meet. Yet we continue to have occasional contact—a letter when you marry, a phone call when you become a parent, and, because Manhattan is so confined, we meet at the theater, shopping at Bloomingdale's, strolling in Central Park, dining in the Village. We gossip a little, perhaps have a drink, embrace and then part. Paul Goodman once said that the purpose of therapy was to turn patients into friends. When we are lucky, then therapy ends, but the life we have forged between us continues.